AN ENQUIRY

INTO THE

ORIGIN OF HONOUR

AN ENQUIRY

INTO THE

ORIGIN OF HONOUR

AND

The Usefulness of
Christianity in War

BERNARD MANDEVILLE

SECOND EDITION

With a new Introduction by

M. M. GOLDSMITH

Professor of Politics, University of Exeter

FRANK CASS & CO. LTD.

1971

Published by
FRANK CASS AND COMPANY LIMITED
67 Great Russell Street, London WC1B 3BT

New Introduction Copyright © 1970   M. M. Goldsmith

First edition   1732
Second edition   1971

ISBN 0 7146 2314 8

c

Printed in Great Britain by Clarke, Doble & Brendon Ltd.
Plymouth and London

INTRODUCTION TO THE ✓
SECOND EDITION

'THAT *Fortitude* has not only a *Rank*, but holds a Place of *Dignity* among *Moral Virtues*, was never contested during the Space of almost Fifty Centuries, till within these four years past.' So contended *An Apology for the Army. In a short Essay on Fortitude* (1715) 'written by an officer', presumably Daniel Defoe. This panegyric on courage was not a response to Bernard Mandeville's *Fable of the Bees*, a book little noticed when it first appeared in 1714. Defoe's pamphlet attacked not Mandeville, but the recently defunct ministry of Robert Harley, Earl of Oxford and Henry St. John, Viscount Bolingbroke, which had denigrated courage and vilified the officers of the British army, especially its Captain-General, the Duke of Marlborough.

But Mandeville was not to be ignored for long. By 1724 the *Fable of the Bees* had become notorious, the success of its second and enlarged edition assured by a grand jury's presenting it as a libel. So when in 1728 Mandeville published a set of dialogues whose only connection to the *Fable* was their similarity of subject, what could have been more appropriate than to call them Part II of the *Fable of the Bees*? An additional set of dialogues between the same principal speakers was published in 1732, the year prior to Mandeville's death; these he called not the *Fable of the Bees, Part III* but *An Enquiry into the Origin of Honour and the Usefulness of Christianity in War.*

Mandeville portrays his speakers in the 'Preface' to Part II of the *Fable*.[1] Horatio is an elegant man of the world, one of the modish 'beau monde', wealthy by birth, an accomplished gentleman. But Horatio is more than a fashionable man of pleasure whose wealth has enabled him to develop exquisite taste in the enjoyment of life. Not only has he acquainted himself with the customs of Europe by travel, he has read widely, particularly in the classics. Being 'altogether disinterested in his Principles', Horatio is capable of carrying on an abstract discussion. He is a worldly rationalist who is entirely sceptical about a personal god, the curious superstitions of Jews and Christians—rather a convinced deist than a perfect atheist. Horatio deviates from Erastianism only to become anti-clerical. As a man of honour, the elegant Horatio dislikes ridicule of valuable social or moral institutions and so depreciates the *Fable of the Bees*.

Horatio's friend, Cleomenes, is also a wealthy gentleman who has travelled. And his reading is even more extensive and more specialized than Horatio's. Not only is he thoroughly familiar with Descartes, Gassendi and Spinoza, but few eighteenth-century gentlemen could have equalled his knowledge of the sciences, especially anatomy. (These characteristics were inherited from his creator; Mandeville had been trained as a Cartesian at the University of Leyden. Taking his M.D. in 1691, Mandeville followed his father and grandfather in specializing in nervous and digestive disorders. Not only did he practise his profession, he even produced a set of dialogues on it—*A Treatise of the Hypocondriack and Hysterick Diseases.*)

Recently, Cleomenes had been engaged in the study of human nature and the examination of his own psychology. In the course of his studies, he came upon the *Fable of the Bees*. Converted, Cleomenes now professes a bizarre concoction of the *Fable* and Christianity which enables him to discover how the baser human characteristics of pride, vanity, greed, flattery and hypocrisy support social institutions. Although he is certain that Christianity is incompatible with seeking the approval of worldly men, gratifying vanity and living in the ease and luxury afforded by one's social position, Cleomenes recognizes that he is incapable of dying to worldly things. His stirrings toward saintliness only serve to make him incapable of renouncing the delights of this world. Understanding what it would be to sacrifice what one likes, to mortify the flesh as a truly religious Christian, he follows St. Augustine and Luther in believing that true Christians are extremely few.

Mandeville explicitly asserts that Cleomenes expresses his views while Horatio does not. But although Cleomenes, who frequently appears as a devoted Protestant of no particular sectarian confession, may usually express Mandeville's own opinion, it is scarcely credible that Horatio never does so. For example, Horatio's telling comparison of Christian with pagan myths and his sceptical attitude toward Christianity represent Mandeville's own views to some degree.[2] And this inference is

supported when Cleomenes' Christianity turns out to approxi-
mate deism with a whiff of revelation.[3] Christianity has mysteries
beyond reason, Cleomenes admits, but its main virtues are that
it made truth more available, more emphatic, and more socially
effective. A dialogue allows its author to present his ideas
dialectically, in a tension between two proponents whom he
never entirely identifies with but never entirely rejects. In Part
II of the *Fable of the Bees*, Horatio and Cleomenes show themselves capable of discussing such disparate subjects as the
relative merits of Dutch and Italian paintings of the Nativity,
the graces of opera, and the character of the Duke of Marlborough as well as examining the psychological and moral
foundations of virtue and honour.

In the *Origin of Honour* Mandeville concentrates his attention not on moral goodness as he had in the *Fable* but on
courage and honour and their relation to religion. Mandeville's
interest in these subjects was neither sudden nor recent. And
the relation between his views and contemporary political debates
is indirect if not elliptical. True, Walpole's government was pursuing a policy of peace toward Spain, France, and the Empire, a
policy that was occasionally denounced by the opposition in
Parliament and in its newspapers such as the *Craftsman*. Bolingbroke's patriotism, echoing Machiavelli, Harrington and the old
Whigs (like John Trenchard and Thomas Gordon who wrote
the *Independent Whig* and *Cato's Letters* in the early 20s),
emphasized the current decadence and corruption of England.
Instead of public spirit, willingness to devote one's time and
energy to the service of the community in an attempt to achieve
the common good, Robinocracy encouraged the pursuit of
political office as a means of serving one's private interests.
Money-grubbing stock-jobbers were ascendant over sturdy
yeomen and honest, independent gentlemen; the moneyed
interest was becoming paramount. No longer was England
defended by her own citizens; instead she relied on a mercenary,
standing army—an expedient well known to endanger liberty.[4]
Mandeville's Private Vices, Publick Benefits, the subtitle of the
Fable of the Bees, challenged this ideology; so did the substance
of Mandeville's ideas for they suggested that the ideal of a
virtuous republic was chimerical for a developed, prosperous
commercial society. It was a model of a primitive and poor
social order. Those who advocated such a model were surely
hypocrites, if they thought it incompatible with prosperity, or

fools, if they were serious. (That they were men of classical virtue was so unlikely on Mandeville's analysis of motives that it could be dismissed.)

Mandeville's attack on the political theory of virtue was mainly indirect. He did not address himself to the specific issues raised; instead, he undermined the theory by showing that vice rather than virtue produced society. Only rarely did Mandeville comment on specifically political matters. When he discussed the qualities necessary for a prime minister, he did Walpole small service. A statesman would have extensive knowledge of history, of the economic geography of various nations, and of their interests and the personalities of their rulers. An expert psychologist, he must be in complete control of himself while he uses his knowledge to penetrate others. But a prime minister needs nothing more than the favour of his prince to put him in power, vanity to make public appearances at which he is idolized a pleasure, common sense and a good memory to give him an adequate grasp of affairs, and health. Above all, he must be unflappable and imperturbable.[5] In short, a man like Sir Robert Walpole will do. And Mandeville makes no effort to magnify Walpole's virtues. Yet his argument legitimizes Walpole's position; to hold that position one need not be the virtuous wise patriot demanded by the opposition; one need not be more than what Sir Robert Walpole is. Walpole is not eulogized nor are Bolingbroke's views supported.

Only occasionally does Mandeville mention subjects that relate unambiguously to the 1720s and 30s. Even his discussion of the prime minister might refer to a previous Robin, Harley, as well as the present one. There have always been prime ministers, asserts Horatio, against Cleomenes' refusal to contemplate officers apart from the constitution.[6] Mandeville's interest in courage and honour extends back to the first part of the *Fable of the Bees* and even beyond. His depreciation of the theory of virtue pre-dates its exposition by Bolingbroke, and even its use by Trenchard and Gordon in their response to the South Sea Bubble. When Cleomenes argues that the chief minister is always extolled by his party and denigrated by the opposition, the example he choses to illustrate this truth is not Robert Walpole, nor even Robert Harley. His example is neither the great minister that Bolingbroke and Swift hated and who drove both of them into exile, nor the one under whom they had their own period of triumph and power, but a man who opposed the Tories in 1710 and whom Swift had vilified in the *Examiner*, John Churchill, Duke of Marlborough.[7] The Tories had ascribed all Marlborough's actions to two motives: ambition and avarice. And no Tory believed this more fervently than Jonathan Swift. Among Marlborough's defenders none was more assiduous than Richard Steele. The Tory campaign against Marlborough was not entirely personal and gratuitous. Marlborough's prestige served the Whigs. The Whigs were committed to a policy of war against Louis XIV until a non-French king was established on the Spanish throne: No peace without Spain. The Tories were prepared to accept Louis' nephew, Philip of Anjou, because the interests of Spain and France were sufficiently divergent to prevent a common policy harmful to England as long as the two crowns were separate. They regarded the aims of the war as having been achieved; they saw no point in England's fighting to impose an unpopular Imperial candidate upon Spain. To undermine Marlborough's prestige was to sap the foundations of the war policy. Marlborough could hardly be accused of incompetence, but it was possible to reflect upon the danger to the constitution from an overly powerful general; it was also possible to accuse Marlborough of wanting the war to continue for sordid and private reasons. Marlborough's pockets were bottomless, his greed unlimited even though he was the greatest and possibly the richest subject. His war profits were already building him a palace, how much more did he want? The Tory policy was peace. To make the Peace of Utrecht the proponents of war had to be overcome. Reasoned argument would be used. But the new weapons of propaganda provided by a communications explosion, an uncensored, uncontrolled, popular press, could be used in other ways as well. Reasoned argument could be effectively supplemented by systematic vilification. So the Whig position was attacked by vilifying Marlborough. Among the casualties of the political battle was Isaac Bickerstaff, Steele's persona in the *Tatler*. The *Tatler* successfully exploited the technical possibility of fairly rapid newspaper production by inventing a new form of journal. It consisted of four columns, two on each side of a sheet fourteen inches by eight inches. It appeared three times a week. Approximately three columns contained the lucubrations (essays, description, reviews and reflections) of Isaac Bickerstaff, Esq., doctor, Oxford graduate, astrologer, and eventually censor of Great Britain; the remainder was filled with short advertisements. The printing press was not a new invention; the newspaper was no innovation. But the *Tatler* was different. What little news it contained in its first few numbers soon disappeared. In its inception it was not partisan; unlike L'Estrange's *Observator* it was not a government's means of scourging the opposition. Bickerstaff was polite, civilized; he meant to instruct and to entertain; he succeeded in being present not only among the gentlemen at the coffee house, but also among the ladies at the tea-table. The *Tatler* invented a new *genre*, the journal of opinion; and it discovered a vast demand for that *genre*. The form was perfected in the *Spectator* and imitated right through the century.

The character of Isaac Bickerstaff had been invented by Swift for an elaborate joke on an almanac maker named Partridge. Purporting to be a rival almanac maker, Bickerstaff criticized the vacuous predictions of 'Partrige'. Among the more precise predictions was the day of Partrige's death. On the subsequent day there appeared a pamphlet account of the demise. The irate Partridge completed the joke by issuing a tendentious denial: he was not dead. He had been alive on March 29, 1708 and he was now alive, a year later. Swift riposited: Partrige had not denied that he died on the day in question—whether he had since revived, let the world judge. Upon reading Partrige's *Almanack* for 1709, several gentlemen had been heard to declare *'They were sure no Man alive ever writ such damned Stuff as this'*.[8] Steele converted the persona to his own use when he started the *Tatler*. When Bickerstaff blundered into party politics, he was abused by the Tories. He eventually had to be killed off. Steele joined Addison in the *Spectator*; Mr. Spectator was less irascible than Bickerstaff, more cool and distant, carefully uninvolved in politics. Later Steele produced the *Guardian*, creating in Nestor Ironsides a staunch Whig. But Bickerstaff was not the only casualty of the political battles of Whig and Tory. His creators destroyed their friendship as each became more committed to his own party.

But before his departure, Isaac Bickerstaff, Esquire, had inspired a considerable number of imitators. One of these was Mrs. Crackenthorpe, the 'lady who knows everything', which she claimed to reveal thrice weekly in the *Female Tatler*. Towards the end of 1709, this paper passed into new hands, those of a 'society of ladies'. Two of the ladies, Lucinda and Artesia wrote approximately half the issues after number 52. These ladies were in fact Bernard Mandeville.

Mandeville's contributions to the *Female Tatler* in 1709–10 are the first full expression of his views. Lucinda and Artesia occasionally reflect on a subject; more frequently they report a conversation. One such report (nos. 62, 64, 66) concerns a discussion about the basis of society. One lady argues that men are passionate and vicious beasts which can be controlled only by repression. Denying this Augustinian or Hobbesian view, Lucinda holds that men have been civilized by public-spirited men who have gradually improved men's morals by acting for the public good and teaching others to do so. This view is indebted to the censorious Esquire Bickerstaff who had generalized the Partridge joke by arguing that all who did not act for the public good or seek to improve themselves were dead and ought to turn themselves in for burial. But the Bickerstaffian position, although it is applauded by the company, does not go unchallenged. In comes an 'Oxford gentleman' who argues that the progress of mankind is not the consequence of conscious, public-spirited benefactors. On the contrary, those do most who, having some wealth, think of nothing but gratifying their desires and inventing new ones. These self-indulgent hedonists inspire others to seek means of pleasing them in return for money. Thus, the necessities, comforts and conveniences of life come to be invented and improved: private vices, public benefits.

Another subject discussed in a series of papers by Captain Steele's Bickerstaff was honour. He condemned the practice of duelling in a series of *Tatlers* beginning with nos. 25–29, 31, 38. Not that Steele wished to disparage honour or courage; he was a strong supporter of the war which was the proper scene for the display of martial virtue. Even this was questioned by Mandeville in a series of papers in which Lucinda and Artesia take opposite sides. They are divided on the question of whether a cousin should follow his two brothers to the war. The father, obsessed with military glory, cannot regard any other possibility with favour although he is neither insensible to the feelings of his wife who has lost two sons and fears to lose the third as well, nor himself untouched with grief. Each of the sisters supports one side; and they call in outside opinion on the question. One party is assisted by Colonel Worthy, the other by our friend, the Oxford gentleman. Eventually Mandeville produces a short poem on the enchantress, Honour:

> In Bloody Fields she Sits as Gay,
> As other Ladies at a Play;

Whilst the Wild Sparks on which she Doats,
Are cutting one another's Throats . . .

The recompense she gives is glory: epitaphs on tombstones that find their way into history, surely pleasing to those chopped down.

But then, they say, the ill-natur'd Jade,
For all her sparks, is still a Maid;
Because none e'er lay in her Bed,
Unless they first were knock'd o' th' head.[9]

Mandeville's concern with courage, honour and religion found its way into the *Fable of the Bees*. Remark C is devoted to a discussion of shame. Shame is the passion precisely opposite to pride; like pride it depends upon a man's opinion of himself. The actions exhibiting shame indicate some consciousness of weakness, inability or guilt. Adopting a modest diffidence toward others can be a mode of flattering them; deference plays upon pride by the pretence that the other person is valued more highly than oneself. Remark R is even more pointed: honour is imaginary, an invention of moralists and politcians to tie men to their commitments. Since a man of honour must be prepared to risk his life for the least injury or affront, he must be possessed of courage. Men like many animals are endowed with a feeling of affection for themselves and consequently a desire to preserve themselves. Apprehending a danger to oneself produces fear. To overcome this passion some other passion is needed: the higher animals have two strong natural appetites, hunger and lust. When one of these is crossed, anger results and anger can for a time overcome fear and the desire for self-preservation. Natural courage has certain disadvantages. To live peacefully in society, men's fears are aroused. Men are conditioned not to use physical violence; their capacity to respond to anger is repressed. Furthermore, those impassioned with anger cannot be disciplined; they are berserk. When this condition passes, as it is likely to do after a short time, only fear remains. So, instead of natural courage, society relies upon artificial courage, playing upon men's pride and shame. Convince some men that they have a praiseworthy and rare passion that allows them to face danger without flinching, and many men will claim this quality. Sooner than be shamed they will face death. To make men fight once artificial courage has been established, it is only necessary to convince them that their cause is just, their interests and objects of love are endangered, and to engage their pride further with a few feathers and by flattering them.[10]

When he returned to the subject in the *Origin of Honour*, Mandeville expanded his account and amended one of its fundamental principles. Where before he had regarded pride and shame as two connected passions, he now held them to be affections of a single passion: self-liking. This is a passion distinct from self-love, the natural desire of the creature for gratifying and preserving itself. Self-liking is innate, a characteristic of the higher animals as well as man; when it is excessive it is called pride; it results in a desire for the approval of others.[11]

Self-liking or self-esteem, is the value men set upon themselves; it varies according to the opinion each man has of himself. To reinforce this opinion men seek the approval of others. The greater the marks of esteem granted, the more the person honoured by them is told to indulge a good opinion of himself. Conversely, to disapprove shows a low opinion of a person; it is an attempt to make him ashamed, to give him a low opinion of his own worth. And approval and disapproval are not distributed in accord with some objective law of good and evil, but according to the norms of some particular group: a gang of thieves disapproves not of theft but of passing up an easy chance.[12]

Being susceptible to the approval of others makes men malleable. Were they morally autonomous creatures, beings whose opinions of themselves were entirely determined by their own judgments of the extent that their actions conformed to the moral law (divine, natural or self-imposed), men might still form societies but they would be vastly different from the societies we know. Men's physical and psychological needs, might force them to combine but they could never be induced to barter real gratification for imaginary. Without that exchange there would be no development of luxury, of the arts and sciences, of commerce, and of morals and manners. Men would remain virtuous but primitive.

Honour has an advantage over virtue as a social reward. Virtue requires real abstinence; honour requires less self-denial —the indulgence of almost all appetites is consistent with honour. A man of honour may override the law, and demand whatever respect he chooses to enforce from others.

But if virtue is insufficient to provide a basis for effective
social obligation, cannot religion do so? Mandeville argues that
religion is necessary. Men naturally believe that there is an
invisible power that causes the unexpected evils that befall
them. This belief is a natural consequence of their passions:
men are born with an aversion to evil or pain. To shun it, they
seek its causes, ascribing to an invisible power any evil whose
origin is unknown. Their Hobbesian natural religion does little
to socialize men. The principal use of men's belief is as a
guarantee of promises and oaths. When a man swears, believing in such a power, we have greater assurance than his mere
affirmation (except for Quakers) can give. But Mandeville has
learned from Bayle's *Miscellaneous Reflections on the Comet*
(secs. 135–139) that the terrors of an eventual reckoning do not
deter sin. Men's natural propensities to believe must be used,
but however sincerely they profess a religion, they are more
likely to be affected by more immediate pains and pleasures.
Neither virtue nor religion, not even Christianity, can supply
the social benefits of honour.

Christianity indeed is directly opposed to honour. Christianity
directs men to humility, patience, resignation and self-denial
rather than to the worship of themselves and the attempt to get
the devotion of others. Christianity forbids revenge, honour
encourages it. Christianity demands forgiveness of those who
injure us; honour forbids it.

True Christianity is thus difficult to practise. No Christian
could accept a challenge, for he risks making himself a mur-
derer for the sake of nothing more than his desire that men
should not think him cowardly. And it's ridiculous to think that
Christianity requires no more austerity and self-denial than to
conform to the ordinary standards of consumption of one's
station in society. While Mandeville denounces the practices of
the Roman Catholics as impostures, he censures the Protestants,
particularly the Church of England for its laxity and indulgence. Protestantism requires that its clergy lead apostolic lives
if they are to be believed; and since it has given up the notion
of infallibility, a Protestant church must expect schisms and be
prepared to tolerate dissent.

On Mandeville's account it is impossible for Christianity to
be useful in war. Superstition and enthusiasm may be useful.
Preachers may play upon men's beliefs to convince them that
God is on their side and against their opponents; they may play

upon small differences in opinions and ceremonies to make men hate each other. Preachers may induce men to fight, but not by preaching the gospel.

Mandeville attempts to purify Christianity by denying its involvement in the affairs of this world. Clever politicians have perverted it to increase men's pride and embitter them against their enemies. Mandeville minimizes the religious fervour of even Cromwell's army; and Cromwell himself becomes an astute politician, possibly without any religion at all. Further, he demonstrates how the sincere and superstitious common soldier may be a wicked man, a degenerate sinner, and yet believe that God is on his side and that his comrades are armed saints.

Mandeville does not believe in wars of religion. He thinks that almost all men are ungodly. If ungodliness and sin are to be extirpated, men must begin by excluding them from their own hearts. But the present constitution of human nature, apart from grace (given to few if any) makes the task hopeless.

Surely Mandeville rejoiced in the impossibility of eradicating sin. He delights in showing that human society is founded on men's needs and that prosperity, comfort, culture and civilization result from men's vices and not from their virtues. Moreover, what passes for virtue in this world, such qualities as courage, benevolence, charity, and piety are far from being what a strict moralist would call virtue. They are nothing but the offspring begot by flattery upon pride. Mandeville offers a dilemma: give up these worldly pleasures or give up hypocrisy. Had he adopted a Biblical motto, he could have taken it from Ecclesiastes, 7, 16: Be not righteous overmuch.

If men forbear judging others, if they examine their own motives as well as those of others, they may come to be less censorious. Taking a 'low view' of human nature means regarding even men's grandest achievements as products of motives men generally disparage. Base motives may produce noble actions; moral judgment cannot be grounded upon the qualities of men's motives.

One alternative is to base evaluation on the consequences of actions. What can be wrong, immoral or evil about any action or any mode of living that does no harm to anyone? Men should not be too censorious of others. If the noble man of courage should not be so highly esteemed, may not the man of commerce, the base money-grubber, be something other than a despicable slave of mammon? If working in his counting-house piling up wealth and abstaining from pleasure is the sort of life a man wishes to lead, can we condemn him for it? Mandeville, as early as the *Female Tatler*, (105, 107, 109 [corrected numbers: 108, 110, 112], March 15, 20, 24, 1710), recognized that men have different desires, wish to live different kinds of lives and should not all be fitted to the same pattern. The miser saves, the prodigal spends, but both may contribute to the prosperity of society.

Mandeville accepted, far more wholeheartedly than many of his contemporaries, the advent of a commercial society. Old Whigs like Trenchard and Gordon, and Tories like Bolingbroke, hated stock-jobbing and money-grubbing. Addison took a contrary view; in the *Spectator* (69, May 19, 1711), he affects to ennoble commerce, finding in the Royal Exchange a prospect of men from all nations contributing to each other's good. It is an emporium for the whole earth filled with ministers of commerce from various nations knitting mankind together by redistributing nature's bounties to the benefit of private individuals and the public. But only Mandeville accepted commerce as commerce. Trade could provide a satisfying way of life for some if not all. It needed no rhetorical embellishment, no pretensions to gentility—it served all men's needs, it provided some men with means convertible to their enjoyment, and for others, however bizarre it might appear to the *beau monde*, trade was itself an enjoyable mode of life. The moral is neatly drawn by Lucinda in *Female Tatler* (109): 'I remember that I was a good big Girl before I could be perswaded, but that they were all Fools that did not love Cheese.'

Demonstrating that all human actions are based on corrupt, sinful, worldly, immoral motives may be intended to evoke one of two different responses. The preacher uses this tactic to remind his hearers of their unworthiness, to show that they can only be saved by throwing themselves on God's mercy. Judged by a righteous God, men are so worthless that they would be hopelessly condemned. A rigoristic standard of morality demonstrates that only by renouncing proud self-reliance and recognizing their inadequacy, thereupon relying on God's love although they do not deserve it, can men be saved. The preacher emphasizes men's sinfulness to evoke repentance.

But if all men's actions are fundamentally sinful has not the preacher undermined his own purpose? Rigorism defines a moral action as one done from a moral motive, such as loving God, doing one's duty, benefiting others, or fulfilling a principle like Kant's categorical imperative. It thus renders suspect any action for an end desired by the actor. To find one's duty pleasant, to like benefiting others, to act for a heavenly reward, to pay attention more to the consequences of actions than to the motives, all disqualify an action from being moral. A clear standard of moral action is provided, but at the price of the systematic doubt that any human action can meet the standard.

As far as anyone can tell, all human actions are humanly motivated, at least tinged with desire for something other than to act rightly. Skeptics may doubt any visible sign of grace or moral rectitude, discovering human motives in all human behaviour. Rigorous Calvinism or Augustinianism can produce a condemnation of human beings so thorough that it caricatures itself. If all men sin all the time, if no man can be righteous, the distinction between good and evil seems meaningless. If men are damned for helping others because they do it as a result of their natural desire to win the approval of other men (approbativeness, a form of pride) and damned for gratifying themselves and ignoring others, damned both if they do and if they don't, then, says the cynic, why not do as you please? Mandeville was completely familiar with Calvinism both Dutch and English. In spite of Mandeville's vehement protests,[13] the worldly cynic leers through the mask of the reforming preacher. But even in his last work, A Letter to Dion, written in answer to Berkeley's Alciphron, Mandeville denies that he is a libertine who favours vice. Berkeley has not read the Fable or he has not read it carefully for if he had he would know that its purpose was rather to expose vice and luxury than commend them. The facts that vice and luxury are essential to worldly prosperity and greatness, that without some degree of natural and moral evil (i.e. human appetites) no society could exist, in no way extenuates that evil.

By showing that prosperity, power and civility were based on luxury and pride, Mandeville confronted the eighteenth century with a set of connected problems that stimulated others to attempt solutions. First, there is the problem of a moral theory. Hume developed one solution to the Mandevilleian problem. He argued that good and evil are human judgments approving or disapproving actions because of their consequences. We judge a moral characteristic good or evil on the same grounds that we judge a natural characteristic good or bad: its tendency to produce results agreeable or disagreeable, useful or harmful, to the person possessing that characteristic or to his associates. If it benefits its possessor and his associates, pride is no vice. Purity of motive is not the ground of moral judgments. They are ultimately derived from human feelings and desires, from pleasure and pain. Hume attempts to explain how judgments of right and wrong, good and evil, differ from simply liking and disliking and how they arise. He and the other utilitarians in effect propose that qualities should not be called vices if they produce what men regard as good.

But there is a rationalist solution to the moral problem as well. For Kant the satisfaction of desire, the pursuit of pleasure or happiness in any of its forms could not provide a moral imperative, but only expedient counsels. Only the good will is good in itself. A moral action is one in which the will is determined by a law, a law legislated for himself by a rational actor. (This is moral autonomy.) Such a law can be formulated in several ways which Kant thought equivalent: (1) Act so that you treat humanity, whether in your own person or in that of another, always as an end and never as a means only; (2) Act as if the maxim of your action were a universal law. The categorical imperative provides a criterion for moral judgment. And although human beings may not have moral autonomy, they can aspire to it. Where Hume developed one side of Mandeville's theory, Kant developed the other.

Mandeville's assertion of a functional relation between vice and prosperity suggested several other modes of thought about the problem of luxury. One of these might be called economic, another historical.

That Mandeville influenced classical economics there is no doubt: Francis Hutcheson and Adam Smith both read at least the *Fable*. There they found an elaborate dissertation on the division of labour: the numerous materials prepared in specialized operations by men all over the world which cooperate in producing scarlet cloth. The unintended consequence of each individual's private desires is a vast complex web of interdependent trading operations. Mandeville explicitly asserts that governments ought not to meddle with traders and he ridicules the notion that a country can improve its trading situation and prosperity by cutting its consumption of foreign luxuries, for how can foreigners pay for the goods they buy of that country but by selling it their goods? When he is arguing annoyingly that the beneficiaries of the great fire of London outnumber the losers, or impudently that thieves, cheats, pickpockets and prostitutes all contribute to the common good, he approaches an economic view of men's relations. Both arguments rest on the premise that every effective demand puts someone to work as a supplier. Every expenditure benefits many, trader, middleman, worker, farmer, landowner, banker or labourer whose services are demanded in the process. And the illegal or immoral source of the money that makes that demand effective is irrelevant. A dress bought by a thief for his whore puts as many people to work as one bought by an honest citizen for his wife.

In discussing these subjects, Mandeville comes close to asserting one of the doctrines of *laissez-faire* economics: the natural harmony of interests. Private vices (the desires, needs and transactions of individuals) left to themselves without any governmental interference, will produce public benefits, the greatest possible amount of wealth. At other times Mandeville seems closer to the more limited notion, held by most of the utilitarians, that men's interests may be artificially harmonized by a prudent government's enactments. By establishing and enforcing rules, governments can make it each person's private interest to promote the good of all—managed by skilful politicians, private vices become public benefits. And Mandeville stipulated that some forms of commerce be encouraged and others discouraged by taxation. If a *laissez-faire* thinker must confine governmental activity to defence, justice (providing a framework of general rules) and public works unsuitable for private entrepreneurs, then Mandeville was not a believer in *laissez-faire*.

Mandeville elusively uses both the natural identity of interests and their artificial identity. When he extolled the benefits derived from crimes like robbery, vices like drunkenness or whoring, and disasters like the great fire, he relied on the natural harmony of interests. But when defending himself against attack, he emphasized the qualifications: he is not recommending vice and crime, he has never denied that they are wrong. No one suggests that men ought to be free from all laws, free to murder, free to steal; no one denies that crimes should be punished, vices rebuked. Here Mandeville relied on the artificial identity of interests, for the clever politician will forbid some things, but turn others to public use—alcoholic liquors debauch their addicts while providing a considerable part of the public revenue.[14]

Mandeville's exploration of the nature and the causes of the wealth of nations was always concerned with exploiting the moral ambiguity of condemning luxury while desiring prosperity. He only approaches the conception of a self-regulating economic system when explaining how the supply of prostitutes will automatically adjust to the demand for them in *A Modest Defence of Publick Stews*.[15]

What Mandeville contributed to the development of classical economics was less a set of specific ideas than a framework of assumptions and problems—a kind of Mandevilleian paradigm. Men have needs. They are motivated to satisfy other men's needs by the desire to satisfy their own. Thus society can be seen as a network of economic exchanges. Furthermore by denying the distinction between necessities and luxuries, Mandeville eliminated one way of distinguishing unacceptable from acceptable economic activity.

The Mandevilleian paradigm set a third problem—the relation between the economic and social institutions of a people and its moral code. When Mandeville suggested that the heroic virtues were appropriate to a Golden Age he was not adopting an attitude of romantic nostalgia. That golden age was an age of primitive rural simplicity. The society he depicted as possessing the overly-praised virtues was a past society, a poor society, a pre-commercial, uncivilized society. To a polite, urban, commercial civilization other modes of conduct are appropriate.

The institutions of any society, its customs, mores, economics, politics, laws, religion, are thus the products of development over time. They are not laid down by founding heroes as those Old Whigs and New Tories held who relied on the tradition of Machiavelli and Harrington, nor are they agreed upon by a group of reasonable compacters establishing a society for themselves, nor are they introduced by public-spirited social benefactors. Social institutions are not produced by conscious and purposeful calculation, nor have they always been just as they are. They are natural without being original and unchanging, conventional without being chosen either arbitrarily or rationally. Social institutions are a result of a long development in which many men, pursuing not the public good, but their own private ends, have participated. Social institutions and mores have been the joint labour of many men over a long period of time.[16]

To ridicule demands for moral reform Mandeville emphasized this historical development of society and morality: commercial prosperity, civility and morality had all developed over time. To demand a return to a rigorous, simple morality was also to suggest a return to a simpler and ruder economy:

> 'they, that would revive
> A Golden Age, must be as free,
> For Acorns, as for Honesty.'

In his original condition, man was not the creature he now has become. Primitive man was an animal, but an animal capable of training himself to live in the various sorts of societies he developed. Different societies have different customs, laws, mores and institutions. This point Montesquieu, a writer heavily indebted to the English neo-Harringtonians as well as to Bodin and Aristotle, was to elaborate at length. But societies also have a history; they develop from primitive savagery through agricultural simplicity to civilized prosperity. There is a pattern in the development of civilizations—they go through a series of stages. This notion, so central to the eighteenth century's notion of history, is inherent in Mandeville's ideas. It appears again and again—in Hume, in Smith, in Rousseau. Indeed, Rousseau's brilliant first discourse 'On the Moral Effects of the Arts and Sciences' is a variation on the theme of luxury. The arts and sciences have developed with the development of civility and prosperity. And this development involved as well the development of vice. Immorality is the price of civilization, and Rousseau affects preferring virtue to civilization. His essay exploits the eighteenth-century obsession with Mandeville's paradox.

Bernard Mandeville, Dutch physician turned English satirist, stung his contemporaries into anger, annoyance or laughter with his pointed 'private vices, publick benefits'. But he also stimulated the best minds of the eighteenth century into dealing with one or another of the problems he suggested. His ideas formed a pattern that every serious thinker encountered and that many found fascinating or puzzling. In this sense, Mandeville's ideas are central to the century.

Were Mandeville merely important we should have to read him. How fortunate that he is fresh, amusing and a great writer as well. Why then has he been so much neglected? High-minded moralizers have always regarded him as rude and crude—unfit to be read by ladies, a rough, low, tavern wit. The charge is partly true, for Mandeville meant to shock the righteous. So he compares eternal moral truths to the statement that it is always wrong to undercook mutton for those who like it done well, and parodies the asceticism of Christianity in a parable about small beer. But Mandeville's ability to discover the telling, direct and homely illustration, his pungent wit, and his obvious delight in stinging the holier-than-thou, make him far more pleasant reading than his highly serious, laboriously graceful, sermonizing contemporaries.

Surely Mandeville is far too little read. Of his major works only the *Fable of the Bees* is readily available—in abbreviated and exerpted versions as well as in F. B. Kaye's elegant and scholarly critical edition. And a few of his shorter works have been reprinted. Putting *An Enquiry into the Origin of Honour and the Usefulness of Christianity in War* once again into print makes one more of Mandeville's books accessible. If any further excuses are needed for doing this I can offer two: first, by doing so we mark the tercentenary of Mandeville's birth, and second, we still need Mandeville's sarcasm to puncture our hypocritical, vain, righteous censoriousness.

M.M.G.

January 1970
University of Exeter

A Note on the Text

The text is reproduced from the only edition, that of 1732. The copy used is in my possession; it collates with copies at the British Museum (2), the Bodleian Library and one loaned to the University of Exeter by the University of Edinburgh. Occasionally copies (British Museum, Columbia University) occur with minor press corrections in signature b.

M.M.G.

NOTES

1 *Fable of the Bees*, edited by F. B. Kaye (2 vols.; Oxford: Clarendon Press, 1924), II, 15–19.
2 *Ibid.*, 306–318.
3 *Origin of Honour*, pp. 25–28.

4 On this subject, see J. G. A. Pocock, 'Machiavelli, Harrington, and English Political Ideologies in the Eighteenth Century', *William and Mary Quarterly* 3rd Series, No. 22 (1965), 549–583, and ' "The Onely Politician": Machiavelli, Harrington and Felix Raab', *Historical Studies: Australia and New Zealand* XII (1966) 265–296; Caroline Robbins *The Eighteenth-Century Commonwealth-man* (Cambridge, Mass.: Harvard University Press, 1959); and most recently Isaac Kramnick, *Bolingbroke and His Circle* (New Haven: Yale University Press, 1969). A selection from Trenchard and Gordon is available in *The English Libertarian Heritage* ed. by David L. Jacobson (Indianapolis: Bobbs-Merrill, 1965); for Bolingbroke see *The Works of Lord Bolingbroke* (4 vols.; Bohn Edition, 1844; reprinted Frank Cass, 1967).

5 *Fable of the Bees*, II, 330–333.

6 *Ibid.*, pp. 325–328. Kaye here makes a rare error by supposing that Walpole was the first to be accused of being a prime minister.

7 *Ibid.*, pp. 336–338.

8 *A Vindication of Isaac Bickerstaff, Esq.* in *The Prose Works of Jonathan Swift* edited by Herbert Davis (14 vols.; Oxford, Basil Blackwell, 1939–1968), II, 162–163; for the whole series of papers see *ibid.*, 141–170.

9 *Female Tatler*, 78, January 4, 1710; see also nos. 77, 80, 84. Mandeville reprinted a revised version in *Wishes to a Godson* (London: J. Baker, 1712), pp. 36–37.

10 *Fable of the Bees*, I, 198–211.

11 *Origin of Honour*, pp. 3–14. Cp., Rousseau's distinction between *amour de soi-même* and *amour propre* in *Discours sur l'inégalité* in the *Political Writings of Jean Jacques Rousseau*, ed. by C. E. Vaughan (2 vols.; Oxford: Basil Blackwell, 1962) I, 217. On these passions see A. O. Lovejoy, *Reflections on Human Nature* (Baltimore: Johns Hopkins, 1961).

12 *Origin of Honour*, p. 10.

13 See his *Vindication* (published in 1723 and included in the edition of the *Fable* that year), *Fable of the Bees* (ed. Kaye), I, 383; and *A Letter to Dion* (London: J. Roberts, 1732 reprinted as Publication Number 41 of the Augustan Reprint Society; Los Angeles: William Andrews Clark Memorial Library, University of California, 1953).

14 *Fable*, I, 85–100; 107–134; 356–359. On Mandeville's relation to *laissez-faire* see Kaye's introduction, *Fable*, I, cxxxiv–cxlvi; Jacob Viner's introduction to *A Letter to Dion*; Nathan Rosenberg, 'Mandeville and laissez-faire', *Journal of the History of Ideas* XXIV (1963), 183–196; and F. A. Hayek, 'Dr. Bernard Mandeville', British Academy lecture on a Master Mind, 1966, *Proceedings of the British Academy* LII (1967), 133–136.

15 *A Modest Defence of Publick Stews: or, an Essay upon whoring, as it is now practis'd in these Kingdoms*, written by a layman. (London: printed by A. Moore, 1724), pp. 61–65. This anonymous work is generally attributed to Mandeville.

16 *Origin of Honour*, pp. 40–41; *Fable*, II, 139–147.

AN
ENQUIRY
INTO
THE ORIGIN
OF
HONOUR,
AND
The Usefulness of
CHRISTIANITY
IN
WAR.

By the Author of the FABLE *of the* BEES.

LONDON:

1732.

THE
PREFACE.

Take it for granted, that a Chriſtian is not bound to believe any Thing to have been of Divine Inſtitution, that has not been declared to be ſuch in Holy Writ. Yet great Offence has been taken at an Eſſay, in the Firſt Part of the Fable of the *Bees,* call'd An Enquiry into the Origin of Moral Virtue ; notwithſtanding the great Caution it is wrote with. Since then, it is thought Criminal to ſurmiſe, that even Heathen Virtue was of Human Invention, and the Reader, in the following Dialogues, will find me to perſiſt in the Opinion, that it was ; I beg his Patience to peruſe what I have to ſay for my ſelf on this Head, which is all I ſhall trouble him with here.

The

The Word *Morality* is either fynonimous with Virtue, or fignifies that Part of Philofophy, which treats of it, and teaches the Regulation of Manners ; and by the Words Moral Virtue, I mean the fame Thing which I believe Every body elfe does. I am likewife fully perfuaded, that to govern our felves according to the Dictates of Reafon, is far better than to indulge the Paffions without Stop or Controul, and confequently that Virtue is more beneficial than Vice, not only for the Peace and real Happinefs of Society in general, but likewife for the Temporal Felicity of every individual Member of it, abftract from the Confideration of a future State. I am moreover convinced, that all wife Men ever were and ever will be of this Opinion ; and I fhall never oppofe Any body, who fhall be pleafed to call this an Eternal Truth.

Having allow'd and own'd thus much, I beg Leave to make a fhort Grammatical Reflection on the Sounds or Letters we make ufe of to exprefs this rational Management of ourfelves : For, tho' the Truth of its Excellency is Eternal, the Words *Moral Virtue* themfelves are not fo, any more than Speech or Man himfelf. Permit me therefore to enquire

which

which Way it is moft probable, they muft have
come into the World.

The Word *Moral*, without Doubt, comes
from *Mos*, and fignifies everyThing that relates
to Manners : The Word *Ethick* is fynonimous
with *Moral*, and is derived from ἔθ©, which
is exactly the fame in *Greek*, that *Mos* is in
Latin. The *Greek* for Virtue, is ἀρετή, which is
derived from ἄρης, the God of War, and proper-
ly fignifies Martial Virtue. The fame Word in
Latin, if we believe *Cicero*, comes from *Vir* ;
and the genuine Signification likewife of the
Word *Virtus* is Fortitude. It is hardly to be
conceived, but that in the firft Forming of all
Societies, there muft have been Struggles for
Superiority ; and therefore it is reafonable to
imagine, that in all the Beginnings of Civil
Government, and the Infancy of Nations,
Strength and Courage muft have been the moft
valuable Qualifications for fome Time. This
makes me think, that *Virtus*, in its firft Ac-
ceptation, might, with great Juftice and Propriety, be in *Englifh* render'd *Manlinefs*; which
fully expreffes the Original Meaning of it, and
fhews the Etymology equally with the *Latin* ;
and whoever is acquainted with that Language muft know, that it was fome Ages before

nonsense

---

fore the *Romans* used it in any other Sense: Nay, to this Day, the Word *Virtus* by it self, in any of their Historians, has the same Signification, as if the Word *Bellica* had been added. We have Reason to think, that, at First, Nothing was meant by *Virtus*, but Daring and Intrepidity, right or wrong; or else it could never have been made to signify Savageness, and brutish Courage; as *Tacitus*, in the Fourth Book of his History, makes use of it manifestly in that Sense. Even Wild Beasts, says he, if you keep them shut up, will lose their Fierceness. *Etiam fera animalia, si clausa teneas, virtutis obliviscuntur.*

What the Great Men of *Rome* valued themselves upon was active and passive Bravery, Warlike Virtue, which is so strongly express'd in the Words of Livy: *Et facere & pati fortia Romanum est.* But besides the Consideration of the great Service, all Warriours receive from this Virtue, there is a very good Reason in the Nature of the Thing it self, why it should be in far higher Esteem than any other. The Passion it has to struggle with, is the most violent and stubborn, and consequently the hardest to be conquer'd, the Fear of Death: The least Conflict with it is harsh Work, and a difficult Task; and it is in

Regard

Regard to this, that *Cicero*, in his *Offices*, calls
Modesty, Justice and Temperance, the softer
and easier Virtues. *Qui virtutibus his leniori-*
bus erit ornatus, modestia, justitia temperan-
tia, &c. Justice and Temperance require
Professors as grave and solemn, and demand as
much Strictness and Observance as any other
Virtues. Why *lenioribus* then ; but that they
are more mild and gentle in the Restraint they
lay upon our Inclinations, and that the Self-
denial they require is more practicable and less
mortifying than that of Virtue itself, as it is
taken in its proper and genuine Sense ? To be
Just or Temperate, we have Temptations to
encounter, and Difficulties to surmount, that
are troublesome : But the Efforts we are oblig'd
to make upon our selves to be truly Valiant are
infinitely greater; and, in order to it, we are
overcome the First, the strongest and most
lasting Passion, that has been implanted in us;
for tho' we may hate and have Aversion to
many Things by Instinct, yet there is Nothing
so generally terrible, and so generally dreadful to all Creatures, rational or not rational, as
the Dissolution of their Being.

Upon due Consideration of what has been
said, it will be easy to imagine, how and why,

soon

soon after Fortitude had been honoured with
the Name of Virtue, all the other Branches
of Conqueſt over our ſelves were dignify'd with
the ſame Title. We may ſee in it likewiſe the
Reaſon of what I have always ſo ſtrenuouſly in-
ſiſted upon, *viz.* That no Practice, no Action
or good Quality, how uſeful or beneficial ſoever
they may be in themſelves, can ever deſerve the
Name of Virtue, ſtrictly ſpeaking, where there
is not a palpable Self-denial to be ſeen. In
Tract of Time, the Senſe of the Word *Virtus*
received ſtill a greater Latitude ; and it ſignify'd Worth, Strength, Authority, and Goodneſs of all Kinds : *Plautus* makes uſe of it, for
Aſſiſtance. *Virtute Deûm*, by the Help of
the Gods. By Degrees it was applied not only
to Brutes, *Eſt in juvencis, eſt in equis patrum
Virtus*, but likewiſe to Things inanimate ;
and was made Uſe of to expreſs the Power, and
peculiar Qualities of Vegetables and Minerals
of all Sorts, as it continues to be to this Day :
The Virtue of the Loadſtone, the Virtue of O-
pium, *&c.* It is highly probable, that the
Word *Moral*, either in *Greek* or *Latin*, never
was thought of before the Signification of the
Word *Virtue* had been extended ſo far beyond its Original ; and then in ſpeaking of the
Virtues

Virtues of our Species, the Addition of that
Epithet became neceſſary, to denote the Rela-
tion they had to our Manners, and diſtinguiſh
them from the Properties and Efficacy of
Plants, Stones, &c. which were likewiſe call'd
Virtues.

If I am wrong, I ſhall be glad to ſee a better
Account, how this Adjective and Subſtantive
came to be join'd together. In the mean Time,
I am very ſure, that there is Nothing ſtrain'd
or forc'd in my Suppoſition. That the Words,
in Tract of Time, are be come of greater Importance, I don't deny. The Words *Clown* and
Villain have opprobrious Meanings annex'd to
them, that were never implied in *Colonus* and
Villanus, from which they were undoubtedly
derived. *Moral*, for ought I know, may now
ſignify *Virtue*, in the ſame Manner and for the
ſame Reaſon, that *Panic* ſignifies *Fear*.

That this Conjecture or Opinion of mine,
ſhould be detracting from the Dignity of *Moral Virtue*, or have a Tendency to bring it into Diſrepute, I can not ſee. I have already
own'd, that it ever was and ever will be pre-
ferable to Vice, in the Opinion of all wiſe
Men. But to call Virtue it ſelf Eternal, can
not be done without a ſtrangely Figurative Way
of

of Speaking.   There is no Doubt, but all Ma-
thematical Truths are Eternal, yet they are
taught; and some of them are very abstruse,
and the Knowledge of them never was acquir'd
without great Labour and Depth of Thought.
Euclid had his Merit ; and it does not appear
that the Doctrine of the *Fluxions* was known
before Sir *Isaac Newton* discover'd that con-
cise Way of Computation ; and it is not impossible that there should be another Method,
as yet unknown, still more compendious, that
may not be found out these Thousand Years.

All Propositions, not confin'd to Time or
Place, that are once true, must be always so;
even in the silliest and most abject Things in the
World ; as for Example, It is wrong to un-
der-roast Mutton for People who love to have
their Meat well done.   The Truth of this,
which is the most trifling Thing I can readily
think on, is as much Eternal, as that of the
Sublimest Virtue.   If you ask me, where this
Truth was, before there was Mutton, or People to dress or eat it, I answer, in the same
Place where Chastity was, before there were
any Creatures that had an Appetite to procreate
their Species. This puts me in Mind of the in-
considerate Zeal of some Men, who, even in
Metaphy-

Metaphyficks, know not how to think abftract-
ly, and cannot forbear mixing their own Meannefs and Imbecillities, with the Idea's they
form of the Supreme Being.

There is no Virtue that has a Name, but it
curbs, regulates, or fubdues fome Paffion that
is peculiar to Humane Nature ; and therefore
to fay, that God has all the Virtues in the
higheft Perfection, wants as much the Apology,
that it is an Expreffion accommodated to vulgar Capacities, as that he has Hands and
Feet, and is angry. For as God has not a Body,
nor any Thing that is Corporeal belonging to
his Effence, fo he is entirely free from Paffions
and Frailties.   With what Propriety then can
we attribute any Thing to him that was invented, or at leaft fignifies a Strength or Ability to conquer or govern Paffions and Frailties ? The Holinefs of God, and all his Per-
fections, as well as the Beatitude he exifts in,
belong to his Nature; and there is no Virtue
but what is acquired.   It fignifies Nothing to
add, that God has thofe Virtues in the higheft
Perfection ; let them be what they will, as to
Perfection, they muft ftill be Virtues ; which,
for the aforefaid Reafons, it is impertinent to
afcribe to the Deity.   Our Thoughts of God
                                                   fhould

fhould be as worthy of him as we are able to frame them ; and as they can not be adequate to his Greatnefs, fo they ought at leaft to be abftract from every Thing that does or can belong to filly, reptile Man : And it is fufficient, whenever we venture to fpeak of a Subject fo immenfly far beyond our Reach, to fay, that there is a perfect and compleat Goodnefs in the Divine Nature, infinitely furpaffing not only the higheft Perfection, which the moft virtuous Men can arrive at, but likewife every Thing that Mortals can conceive about it.

I recommend the fore-going Paragraph to the Confideration of the Advocates for the Eternity and Divine Original of Virtue; affuring them, that, if I am miftaken, it is not owing to any Perverfenefs of my Will, but Want of Underftanding.

The Opinion, that there can be no Virtue without Self-denial, is more advantagious to Society than the contrary Doctrine, which is a vaft Inlet to Hypocrify, as I have fhewn at large † : Yet I am willing to allow, that Men may contract a Habit of Virtue, fo as to practife it, without being fenfible of Self-denial, and

---

† Fable of the *Bees.* p. 11. P. 106.

even

even that they may take Pleasure in Actions
that would be impracticable to the Vicious:
But then it is manifest, that this Habit is the
Work of Art, Education and Custom; and it
never was acquired, where the Conquest over
the Passions had not been already made. There
is no Virtuous Man of Forty Years, but he may
remember the Conflict he had with some Appetites before he was Twenty. How natural
seem all Civilities to be to a Gentleman! Yet
Time was, that he would not have made his
Bow, if he had not been bid.

Whoever has read the Second Part of the
Fable of the *Bees*, will see, that in these Dialogues I make Use of the same Persons, who
are the Interlocutors there, and whose Characters have been already drawn in the Preface
of that Book.

THE
CONTENTS
OF THE
First Dialogue.

The CONTENTS.

The

The CONTENTS.

The Contents of the Second Dialogue.

The

The CONTENTS.

The CONTENTS.

The

The CONTENTS.

The Contents of the Third Dialogue.

                                              In—

The CONTENTS.

The CONTENTS.

The Contents of the Fourth Dialogue.

                                              The

The CONTENTS.

ERRATA.

Page 81. Line 6. *read* Influence. P. 94. l. 12. *r.* Proprætors. P. 174. l. 3. *r.* Rites.

THE

[1]

THE
First Dialogue
BETWEEN
Horatio and *Cleomenes.*

Horatio.

Wonder you never attempted to guefs at the Origin of Honour, as you have done at that of Politenefs, and your Friend in his Fable of the Bees has done at the Origin of Virtue.

Cleo. I have often thought of it, and am fatisfied within my felf, that my Conjecture about it is Juft; but there are Three fubftantial Reafons, why I have hitherto kept it to my Self, and never yet mention'd to any One,

what

what my Sentiments are concerning the Origin of that charming Sound.

Hor. Let me hear your Reasons however.

Cleo. The Word Honour, is used in such different Acceptations, is now a Verb, then a Noun, sometimes taken for the Reward of Virtue, sometimes for a Principle that leads to Virtue, and, at others again, signifies Virtue it self; that it would be a very hard Task to take in every Thing that belongs to it, and at the same Time avoid Confusion in Treating of it. This is my First Reason. The Second is: That to set forth and explain my Opinion on this Head to others with Perspicuity, would take up so much Time, that few People would have Patience to hear it, or think it worth their while to bestow so much Attention, as it would require, on what the greatest Part of Mankind would think very trifling.

Hor. This Second whets my Curiosity : pray, what is your Third Reason?

Cleo. That the very Thing, to which, in my Opinion, Honour owes its Birth, is a Passion in our Nature, for which there is no Word coin'd yet, no Name that is commonly known and receiv'd in any Language.

Hor. That is very strange.

Cleo.

Cleo. Yet not lefs true. Do you remember what I faid of Self-liking in our Third Converfation. when I fpoke of the Origin of Politenefs ?

Hor. I do ; but you know, I hate Affectation and Singularity of all Sorts. Some Men are fond of uncouth Words of their own making, when there are other Words already known, that found better, and would equally explain their Meaning : What you call'd then Self-liking at laft prov'd to be Pride, you know.

Cleo. Self-liking I have call'd that great Value, which all Individuals fet upon their own Perfons ; that high Efteem, which I take all Men to be born with for themfelves. I have proved from what is conftantly obferv'd in Suicide, that there is fuch a Paffion in Human Nature, and that it is plainly * diftinct from Self-love. When this Self-liking is exceffive, and fo openly fhewn as to give Offence to others, I know very well it is counted a Vice and call'd Pride : But when it is kept out of Sight, or is fo well difguis'd as not to appear in its own Colours, it has no Name, tho' Men act from that and no other Principle.

---

* Fable of the Bees, part II. p. 141.

Hor.

Hor. When what you call Self-liking, that just Esteem which Men have naturally for themselves, is moderate, and spurs them on to good Actions, it is very laudable, and is call'd the Love of Praise or a Desire of the Applause of others. Why can't you take up with either of these Names?

Cleo. Because I would not confound the Effect with the Cause. That Men are desirous of Praise, and love to be applauded by others, is the Result, a palpable Consequence, of that Self-liking which reigns in Human Nature, and is felt in every one's Breast before we have Time or Capacity to reflect and think of Any body else. What Moralists have taught us concerning the Passions, is very superficial and defective. Their great Aim was the Publick Peace, and the Welfare of the Civil Society; to make Men governable, and unite Multitudes in one common Interest.

Hor. And is it possible that Men can have a more noble Aim in Temporals?

Cleo. I don't deny that; but as all their Labours were only tending to those Purposes, they neglected all the rest; and if they could but make Men useful to each other and easy to themselves, they had no Scruple about the

Means

Means they did it by, nor any Regard to Truth or the Reality of Things; as is evident from the grofs Abfurdities they have made Men fwallow concerning their own Nature, in fpight of what All felt within. In the Culture of Gardens, whatever comes up in the Paths is weeded out as offenfive and flung upon the Dunghill; but among the Vegetables that are all thus promifcuoufly thrown away for Weeds, there may be many curious Plants, on the Ufe and Beauty of which a Botanift would read long Lectures. The Moralifts have endeavour'd to rout Vice, and clear the Heart of all hurtful Appetites and Inclinations : We are beholden to them for this in the fame Manner as we are to Thofe who deftroy Vermin, and clear the Countries of all noxious Creatures. But may not a Naturalift diffect Moles, try Experiments upon them, and enquire into the Nature of their Handicraft, without Offence to the Mole-catchers, whofe Bufinefs it is only to kill them as faft as they can ?

Hor. What Fault is it you find with the Moralifts ? I can't fee what you drive at.

Cleo. I would fhew you, that the Want of Accuracy in them, when they have treated of

H t-

Human Nature, makes it extremely difficult to speak intelligibly of the different Faculties of our intellectual Part. Some Things are very essential, and yet have no Name, as I have given an Instance in that Esteem which Men have naturally for themselves, abstract from Self-love, and which I have been forced to coin the Word Self-liking for : Others are miscall'd and said to be what they are not. So most of the Passions are counted to be Weaknesses, and commonly call'd Frailties; whereas they are the very Powers that govern the whole Machine ; and, whether they are perceived or not, determine or rather create the Will that immediately precedes every deliberate Action.

Hor. I now understand perfectly well what you mean by Self-liking. You are of Opinion, that we are all born with a Passion manifestly distinct from Self-love; that, when it is moderate and well regulated, excites in us the Love of Praise, and a Desire to be applauded and thought well of by others, and stirs us up to good Actions : but that the same Passion, when it is excessive, or ill turn'd, whatever it excites in our Selves, gives Offence to others, renders us odious, and is call'd Pride.

Pride. As there is no Word or Expreſſion that comprehends all the different Effects of this ſame Cauſe, this Paſſion, you have made one, *viz.* Self-liking, by which you mean the Paſſion in general, the whole Extent of it, whether it produces laudable Actions, and gains us Applauſe, or ſuch as we are blamed for and draw upon us the ill Will of others.

Cleo. You are extremely right ; this was my Deſign in coining the Word Self-liking.

Hor. But you ſaid, that Honour owes its Birth to this Paſſion; which I don't underſtand, and wiſh you would explain to me.

Cleo. To comprehend this well, we ought to conſider, that as all Human Creatures are born with this Paſſion, ſo the Operations of it are manifeſtly obſerved in Infants, as ſoon as they begin to be conſcious and to reflect, often before they can ſpeak or go.

Hor. As how ?

Cleo. If they are praiſed, or commended, tho' they don't deſerve it, and good Things are ſaid of them, tho' they are not true, we ſee, that Joy is raiſed in them, and they are pleaſed : On the Contrary, when they are reproved and blamed, tho' they know themſelves to be in Fault, and bad Things are ſaid of the n

them, tho' Nothing but Truth, we fee it excites Sorrow in them and often Anger. This
Paffion of Self-liking, then, manifefting it felf
fo early in all Children that are not Idiots, it is
inconceivable that Men fhould not be fenfible,
and plainly feel, that they have it long before
they are grown up: And all Men feeling
themfelves to be affected with it, tho' they
know no Name for the Thing it felf, it is impoffible, that they fhould long converfe together in Society without finding out, not only that others are influenced with it as well as
themfelves, but likewife which Way to pleafe
or difpleafe one another on Account of this
Paffion.

Hor. But what is all this to Honour?

Cleo. I'll fhew you. When *A* performs
an Action which, in the Eyes of *B*, is laudable,
B wifhes well to *A*; and, to fhew him his Satisfaction, tells him, that fuch an Action is an
Honour to Him, or that He ought to be Honoured for it: By faying this, *B*, who knows
that all Men are affected with Self-liking, in-
tends to acquaint *A*, that he thinks him in
the Right to gratify and indulge himfelf in
the Paffion of Self-liking. In this Senfe the
Word Honour, whether it is ufed as a Noun

or

or a Verb, is always a Compliment we make to Thofe who act, have, or are what we approve of; it is a Term of Art to exprefs our Concurrence with others, our Agreement with them in their Sentiments concerning the Efteem and Value they have for themfelves. From what I have faid, it muft follow, that the greater the Multitudes are that exprefs this Concurrence, and the more expenfive, the more operofe, and the more humble the Demonftrations of it are, the more openly likewife they are made, the longer they laft, and the higher the Quality is of Thofe who join and affift in this Concurrence, this Compliment; the greater, without all Difpute, is the Honour which is done to the Perfon in whofe Favour thefe Marks of Efteem are difplay'd: So that the higheft Honour which Men can give to Mortals, whilft alive, is in Subftance no more, than the moft likely and moft effectual Means that HumanWit can invent to gratify, ftir up, and encreafe in Him, to whom that Honour is paid, the Paffion of Self-liking.

Hor. I am afraid it is true.

Cleo. To render what I have advanced more confpicuous, we need only look into the Reverfe of Honour, which is Difhonour

or

or Shame, and we shall find, that this could
have had no Exiftence any more than Honour, if there had not been fuch a Paffion in
our Nature as Self-liking. When we fee
Others commit fuch Actions, as are vile and
odious in our Opinion, we fay, that fuch
Actions are a Shame to them, or that they
ought to be afhamed of them. By this
we fhew, that we differ from them in their
Sentiments concerning the Value which we
know, that they, as well as all Mankind,
have for their own Perfons; and we are endeavouring to make them have an ill Opinion
of themfelves, and raife in them that fincere
Sorrow, which always attends Man's reflecting on his own Unworthinefs. I defire, you
would mind, that the Actions which we thus
condemn as vile and odious, need not to be fo
but in our own Opinion; for what I have
faid happens among the worft of Rogues, as
well as among the better Sort of People. If one
Villain fhould neglect picking a Pocket, when
he might have done it with Eafe, another of
the fame Gang, who was near him and faw
this, would upbraid him with it in good Earneft, and tell him, that he ought to be afhamed of having flipt fo fair an Opportunity.

Some-

Sometimes Shame fignifies the vifible Diforders that are the Symptoms of this forrowful
Reflection on our own Unworthinefs; at
others, we give that Name to the Punifhments
that are inflicted to raife thofe Diforders; but
the more you will examine into the Nature of
either, the more you will fee the Truth of
what I have afferted on this Head; and all
the Marks of Ignominy, that can be thought
of, have a plain Tendency to mortify Pride;
which, in other Words, is to difturb, take away
and extirpate every Thought of Self-liking.

Hor. The Author of the Fable of the *Bees,*
I think, pretends fomewhere to fet down
the different Symptoms of Pride and Shame.

Cleo. I believe they are faithfully copied
from Nature. —— Here is the Paffage; pray
read it.

Hor. * *When a Man is overwhelm'd with
Shame, he obferves a Sinking of the Spirits; the
Heart feels cold and condenfed, and the Blood
flies from it to the Circumference of the Body;
the Face glows; the Neck and part of the Breaft
partake of the Fire: He is heavy as Lead; the
Head is hung down; and the Eyes through a*

---

* Fable of the Bees, Page 57.

Mift

*Mist of Confusion are fix'd on the Ground : No
Injuries can move him ; he is weary of his Being,
and heartily wishes he could make himself invisible : But when, gratifying his Vanity, he exults in his Pride, he discovers quite contrary
Symptoms ; his Spirits swell and fan the Arterial Blood ; a more than ordinary Warmth
strengthens and dilates the Heart ; the Extremities are cool ; he feels Light to himself, and
imagines he could tread on Air ; his Head is held
up ; his Eyes are roll'd about with Sprightliness ;
he rejoices at his Being, is prone to Anger, and
would be glad that all the World could take
Notice of him.*

Cleo. That's all.

Hor. But you see, he took Pride and Shame
to be two distinct Passions; nay, in another
Place he has call'd them so.

Cleo. He did; but it was an Errour, which
I know he is willing to own.

Hor. What he is willing to own I don't
know ; but I think he is in the Right in what
he says of them in his Book.   The Symptoms
of Pride and Shame are so vastly different,
that to me it is inconceivable, they should
proceed from the same Passion.

Cleo.

Cleo. Pray think again with Attention, and you'll be of my Opinion. My Friend compares the Symptoms that are obferved in Human Creatures when they exult in their Pride, with thofe of the Mortification they feel when they are overwhelm'd with Shame. The Symptoms, and if you will the Senfations, that are felt in the Two Cafes, are, as you fay, vaftly different from one another; but no Man could be affected with either, if he had not fuch a Paffion in his Nature, as I call Self-liking. Therefore they are different Affections of one and the fame Paffion, that are differently obferved in us, according as we either enjoy Pleafure, or are aggriev'd on Account of that Paffion; in the fame Manner as the moft happy and the moft miferable Lovers are happy and miferable on the Score of the fame Paffion. Do but compare the Pleafure of a Man, who with an extraordinary Appetite is feafting on what is delicious to him, to the Torment of another, who is extremely hungry, and can get Nothing to eat. No Two Things in the World can be more different, than the Pleafure of the One is from the Torment of the other; yet Nothing is more evident, than that both

are

are derived from and owing to the fame craving Principle in our Nature, the Defire of Food; for when this is entirely loft, it is more vexatious to eat, than it is to let it alone, tho' the whole Body languifhes, and we are ready to expire for Want of Suftenance. Hitherto I have fpoken of Honour in its firft literal Senfe, in which it is a Technic Word in the Art of Civility, and fignifies a Means which Men by Converfing together have found out to pleafe and gratify one another on Account of a palpable Paffion in our Nature, that has no Name, and which therefore I call Self-liking. In this Senfe I believe the Word Honour, both as a Verb and a Noun, to be as Ancient as the oldeft Language. But there is another Meaning befides, belonging to the fame Sound; and Honour fignifies likewife a Principle of Courage, Virtue, and Fidelity, which fome Men are faid to act from, and to be aw'd by, as others are by Religion. In this latter Senfe, it is much more modern, and I don't believe to be met with a Thoufand Years ago in any Language.

Hor. How! Is it but within thefe Thoufand Years that there have been Men of Bravery and Virtue? Have not the *Greeks* and

Ro-

Romans had great Numbers of them? Were not the *Horatii* and *Curiatii* Men of Honour?

Cleo. They never were call'd fo. All Ages and moſt Countries have produced Men of Virtue and Bravery; but this I do not enquire into now: What I aſſert to be modern is the Phraſe, the Term of Art; it is that which the Ancients knew Nothing of; nor can you with Ten Words, in either *Greek* or *Latin,* expreſs the entire Idea which is annex'd to the Word Honour when it ſignifies a Principle. To be a Man of Honour, it is not ſufficient, that he, who aſſumes that Title, is brave in War, and dares to fight againſt the Enemies of his Country; but he muſt likewiſe be ready to engage in private Quarrels, tho' the Laws of God and his Country forbid it. He muſt bear no Affront without reſenting it, nor refuſe a Challenge, if it be ſent to him in a proper Manner by a Man of Honour. I make no Doubt, but this Signification of the Word Honour is entirely Gothick, and ſprung up in ſome of the moſt ignorant Ages of Chriſtianity. It ſeems to have been an Invention to influence Men, whom Religion had no Power over. All Human Creatures have a reſtleſs Deſire of mending

ding

ding their Condition; and in all Civil Societies and Communions of Men there seems to
be a Spirit at Work, that, in Spight of the
continual Opposition it receives from Vice
and Misfortunes, is always labouring for, and
seeking after what can never be obtain'd
whilst the World stands.

Hor. What is that pray?

Cleo. To make Men compleatly Happy
upon Earth. Thus Men make Laws to ob-
viate every Inconveniency they meet with;
and as Times discover to them the Insuffi-
ciency of those Laws, they make others with
an Intent to enforce, mend, explain or repeal
the former; till the Body of Laws grows to
such an enormous Bulk, that to understand it
is a tedious prolix Study, and the Numbers
that follow and belong to the Practise of it,
come to be a Grievance almost as great as
could be fear'd from Injustice and Oppression.
Nothing is more necessary, than that Property
should be secured; and it is impossible but
on many Occasions Men must trust one another in the Civil Society. Now Nothing has
ever been thought to be more obligatory or a
greater Tie upon Man than Religion.

Hor.

Hor. This I have often wonder'd at: Considering the Abſurdities in the Religion of the *Greeks* and *Romans*, the bad Examples and Immoralities of their Deities, the ridiculous Fables of a *Charon*, a *Styx*, a *Cerberus*, &c, and the Obſcenity diſplay'd in ſeveral of their Feſtivals, I cannot conceive how Men could expect, that ſuch Religions ſhould make Men Honeſt, or do any good to their Morals ; and yet, which is amazing to me, moſt wiſe Men in all Ages have agreed, that, without ſome Religion or other, it would be impoſſible to govern any conſiderable Nation. However, I believe it is Fact, that it never was done.

Cleo. That no large Society of Men can be well govern'd without Religion, and that there never was a Nation that had not ſome Worſhip, and did not believe in ſome Deity or other, is moſt certain : But what do you think is the Reaſon of that?

Hor. Becauſe Multitudes muſt be aw'd by Something that is terrible, as Flames of Hell, and Fire everlaſting ; and it is evident, that if it was not for the Fear of an After-Reckoning, ſome Men would be ſo wicked, that there would be no living with them.

Cleo. Pray, how wicked would they be? What Crimes would they commit?

Hor. Robbing, Murdering, Raviſhing.

Cleo. And are not often here, as well as in other Nations, People convicted of, and puniſh'd for thoſe Crimes?

Hor. I am ſatisfied, the Vulgar could not be managed without Religion of ſome Sort or other; for the Fear of Futurity keeps Thouſands in Awe, who, without that Reflection, would all be guilty of thoſe Crimes which are now committed only by a Few.

Cleo. This is a Surmiſe without any Foundation. It has been ſaid a Thouſand Times by Divines of all Sects; but No body has ever ſhewn the leaſt Probability of its being true; and daily Experience gives us all the Reaſon in the World to think the Contrary; for there are Thouſands, who, throughout the Courſe of their Lives, ſeem not to have the leaſt Regard to a future State, tho' they are Believers; and yet theſe very People are very cautious of committing any Thing which the Law would puniſh. You'll give me Leave to obſerve by the By, that to believe what you ſay, a Man muſt have a worſe Opinion of his Species, than ever the Author of the *Fable of the Bees* appears to have had yet.

　　　　　　　　　　　　　　　　　Hor.

Hor. Don't miſtake me: I am far from believing, that Men of Senſe and Education
are to be frighten'd with thoſe Bugbears.

Cleo. And what I ſay, I don't mean of Li-
bertines or Deiſts ; but Men, that to all outward Appearance are Believers, that go to
Church, receive the Sacrament, and at the
Approach of Death are obſerved to be really
afraid of Hell. And yet of theſe, many are Drun-
kards, Whoremaſters, Adulterers, and not a
Few of them betray their Truſt, rob their
Country, defraud Widows and Orphans, and
make wronging their Neighbours their daily
Practice.

Hor. What Temporal Benefit can Religion
be of to the Civil Society, if it don't keep People in Awe?

Cleo. That's another Queſtion. We both
agree, that no Nation or large Society can be
well govern'd without Religion. I ask'd you
the Reaſon of this : You tell me, becauſe the
Vulgar could not be kept in Awe without it.
In Reply to this, I point at a Thouſand Inſtan-
ces, where Religion is not of that Efficacy,
and ſhew you withal, that this End of keeping
Men in Awe is much better obtain'd by the
Laws and temporal Puniſhment; and that it is
the

the Fear of them, which actually restrains
great Numbers of wicked People; I might say
All, without Exception, of whom there is any
Hope or Possibility, that they can be curb'd
at all, or restrain'd by any Thing whatever:
For such Reprobates as can make a Jest of the
Gallows, and are not afraid of Hanging, will
laugh likewise at Hell and defy Damnation.

Hor. If the Reason I alledge is insufficient,
pray give me a better.

Cleo. I'll endeavour it. The First Business
of all Governments, I mean the Task which
all Rulers must begin with, is, to make
Men tractable and obedient, which is not
to be perform'd, unless we can make them
believe, that the Instructions and Commands
we give them have a plain Tendency to
the Good of every Individual, and that we
say Nothing to them, but what we know
to be true. To do this effectually, Human
Nature ought to be humour'd as well as
studied : Whoever therefore takes upon him
to govern a Multitude, ought to inform himself of those Sentiments that are the natural
Result of the Passions and Frailties which every Human Creature is born with.

Hor. I don't understand what Sentiments
you speak of.

Cleo.

Cleo. I'll explain my felf. All Men are born with Fear; and as they are likewife born with a Defire of Happinefs and Self-Prefervation, it is natural for them to avoid Pain and every Thing that makes them uneafy; and which, by a general Word, is call'd Evil. Fear being that Paffion which infpires us with a ftrong Averfion to Evil, it is very natural to think that it will put us upon enquiring into the Means to fhun it. I have told you already, in our Fifth Converfation, how this Averfion to Evil, and Endeavour to fhun it, this Principle of Fear, would always naturally difpofe Human Creatures to fufpect the Exiftence of an intelligent Caufe that is invifible, whenever any Evil happen'd to them, which came they knew not whence, and of which the Author was not to be feen. If you remember what I faid then, the Reafons why no Nations can be govern'd without Religion, will be obvious. Every Individual, whether he is a Savage, or is born in a Civil Society, is perfuaded within, that there is fuch an invifible Caufe; and fhould any Mortal contradict this, no Multitude would believe a Word of what he faid. Whereas, on the other Hand, if a Ruler humours this

this Fear, and puts it out of all Doubt, that
there is such an invisible Cause, he may
say of it what he pleases; and no Multitude,
that was never taught any Thing to the contrary, will ever dispute it with him. He
may say, that it is a Crocodile or a Monkey,
an Ox, or a Dog, an Onion, or a Wafer. And
as to the Essence and the Qualities of the invisible Cause, he is at Liberty to call it
very good or very bad. He may say of it,
that it is an envious, malicious, and the most
cruel Being that can be imagin'd; that it
loves Blood, and delights in Human Sacrifices: Or he may say, that there are two invisible Causes; one the Author of Good, the
other of Evil; or that there are Three; or
that there is really but One, tho' seemingly
there are Three, or else that there are Fifty
Thousand. The many Calamities we are lia-
ble to, from Thunder and Lightning, Hur-
ricanes and Earthquakes, Plagues and Inunda-
tions, will always make ignorant and un-
taught Men more prone to believe, that the
invisible Cause is a bad mischievous Being,
than that it is a good benign one; as I shew'd
you then in that Fifth Conversation.

Hor. On this Head I own I must give up
Man-

Mankind, and cannot maintain the Excellency of Human Nature; for the Abſurdities in Idolatrous Worſhip, that have been and are ſtill committed by ſome of our own Species, are ſuch as no Creatures of any other could out-do them in.

Cleo. The Proteſtant and the Mahometan are the only National Religions now, that are free from Idolatry; and therefore the Abſurdities in the Worſhip of all the Reſt are pretty much alike; at leaſt, the Difference in the Degrees of Mens Folly, as Idolaters, is very inconſiderable. For how unknown ſoever an inviſible Cauſe, Power, or Being may be, that is incomprehenſible, this is certain of it, that no clear intelligible Idea can be form'd of it; and that no Figure can deſcribe it. All Attempts then, to repreſent the Deity, being equally vain and frivolous, no One Shape or Form can be imagin'd of it, that can juſtly be ſaid to be more or leſs abſurd than another. As to the temporal Benefit which Religion can be of to the Civil Society, or the Political View which Lawgivers and Governours may have in promoting it, the chief Uſe of it is in Promiſes of Allegiance and Loyalty, and all ſolemn Engagements and Aſſeverations, in which the inviſible Power, that, in eve-

every Country, is the Object of the Public k
Worſhip, is invoked or appeal'd to. For theſe
Purpoſes all Religions are equally ſerviceable;
and the worſt is better than none : For without
the Belief of an inviſible Cauſe, no Man's
Word is to be relied upon, no Vows or Pro-
teſtations can be depended upon ; but as ſoon
as a Man believes, that there is a Power ſome-
where, that will certainly puniſh him, if he
forſwears himſelf ; as ſoon, I ſay, as a Man
believes this, we have Reaſon to truſt to his
Oath; at leaſt, it is a better Teſt than any other
Verbal Aſſurance. But what this ſame Perſon
believes further, concerning the Nature and the
Eſſence of that Power he ſwears by, the Worſhip it requires, or whether he conceives it in
the ſingular or plural Number, may be very
material to himſelf, but the Society has Nothing to do with it : Becauſe it can make no
Alteration in the Security which his Swearing
gives us. I don't deny the Uſefulneſs which
even the worſt Religion that can be, may be
of to Politicians and the Civil Society: But
what I inſiſt upon, is, that the temporal Benefit of it, or the Contrivance of Oaths and
Swearing, could never have enter'd into the
Heads of Politicians, if the Fear of an inviſible

fible Caufe had not pre-exifted and been fuppofed to be univerfal, any more than they
would have contrived Matrimony, if the Defire of Procreation had not been planted in
Human Nature and vifible in both Sexes. Paffions don't affect us, but when they are provo-
ked: The Fear of Death is a Reality in our
Nature: But the greateft Cowards may, and
often do, live Forty Years and longer, without
being difturb'd by it. The Fear of an invifible Caufe is as real in our Nature, as the
Fear of Death; either of them may be conquer'd perhaps; but fo may Luft; and Experience teaches us, that how violent foever the
Defire of Propagating our Species may be
whilft we are young, it goes off, and is often
entirely loft in old Age. When I hear a Man
fay, that he never felt any Fear of an invifible
Caufe, that was not owing to Education, I
believe him as much as I do a young married
Woman in Health and Vigour, who tells me,
that fhe never felt any Love to a Man, that did
not proceed from a Senfe of her Duty.

Hor. Does this Fear, this Acknowledgment
of an invifible Caufe, difpofe or excite Men
any more to the true Religion, than it does to
the groffeft and moft abominable Idolatry?

Cleo.

Cleo. I don't say it does. But there is no Paffion in Human Nature fo beneficial, that, according as it is managed, may not do Mifchief as well as good. What do you think of Love ? If this Fear had not been common to the whole Species, none could have been influenc'd by it ; the Confequence of which muft have been, that Men would have rejected the true Religion as well as the falfe. There is Nothing that Men may differ in, in which they will ever be all of the fame Opinion: And abftrufe Truths do often feem to be lefs probable than well drefs'd Fables, when they are skilfully accommodated to our Underftanding, and agreeable to our own Way of thinking. That there is but one God, the Creator of Heaven and Earth, that is an all-wife and perfectly good Being, without any Mixture of Evil, would have been a moft rational Opinion, tho' it had not been reveal'd. But Reafoning and Metaphyficks muft have been carried on to a great Height of Perfection, before this Truth could be penetrated into by the Light of Nature. *Plutarch*, who was a Man of great Learning, and has in many Things difplay'd good Senfe and Capacity, thought it impoffible, that one Being fhould

have

have been the Cause of the Whole, and was therefore of Opinion, that there muſt have been Two Principles; the one to produce all the Good; and the other all the Evil that is in the World. And Some of the greateſt Men have been of this Opinion, both before and ſince the Promulgation of the Goſpel. But whatever Philoſophers and Men of Letters may have advanced, there never was an Age or a Country where the Vulgar would ever come into an Opinion that contradicted that Fear, which all Men are born with, of an inviſible Cauſe, that meddles and interferes in Human Affairs; and there is a greater Poſſibility, that the moſt Senſeleſs Enthuſiaſt ſhould make a knowing and polite Nation believe the moſt incredible Falſities, or that the moſt odious Tyrant ſhould perſuade them to the groſſeſt Idolatry, than that the moſt artful Politician, or the moſt popular Prince, ſhould make Atheiſm to be univerſally received among the Vulgar of any conſiderable State or Kingdom, tho' there were no Temples or Prieſts to be ſeen. From all which I would ſhew, that, on the one Hand, you can make no Multitudes believe contrary to what they feel, or what contradicts a Paſſion inhe-

rent

rent in their Nature, and that, on the other, if you humour that Paſſion, and allow it to be juſt, you may regulate it as you pleaſe. How unanimous ſoever, therefore, all Rulers and Magiſtrates have ſeem'd to be in promoting ſome Religion or other, the Principle of it was not of their Invention. They found it in Man; and the Fear of an inviſible Cauſe being univerſal, if Governours had ſaid Nothing of it, every Man in his own Breaſt would have found Fault with them, and had a Superſtition of his own to himſelf. It has often been ſeen, that the moſt ſubtle Unbelievers among Politicians have been forced, for their own Quiet, to counterfeit their Attachment to Religion, when they would a Thouſand Times rather have done without it.

Hor. It is not in the Power then, you think, of Politicians to contradict the Paſſions, or deny the Exiſtence of them, but that, when once they have allow'd them to be juſt and natural, they may guide Men in the Indulgence of them, as they pleaſe.

Cleo. I do ſo; and the Truth of this is evident likewiſe in another Paſſion, (*viz*) that of Love, which I hinted at before; and Marriage was not invented to make Men procreate;

ate; they had that Defire before; but it was inftituted to regulate a ftrong Paffion, and prevent the innumerable Mifchiefs that would enfue, if Men and Women fhould converfe together promifcuoufly, and love and leave one another as Caprice and their unruly Fancy led them. Thus we fee, that every Legiflator has regulated Matrimony in that Way, which, to the beft of his Skill, he imagin'd would be the moft proper to promote the Peace and Felicity in general of Thofe he govern'd: And how great an Impoftor foever *Mahomet* was, I can never believe, that he would have allow'd his *Muffulmen* Three or Four Wives a piece, if he had thought it better, that one Man fhould be contented with and confin'd to One Woman ; I mean better upon the Whole, more beneficial to the Civil Society, as well in Confideration of the Climate he lived in, as the Nature and the Temperament of thofe *Arabians* he gave his Laws to.

Hor. But what is all this to the Origin of Honour? What Reafon have you to think it to be of Gothick Extraction ?

Cleo. My Conjecture concerning Honour, as it fignifies a Principle from which Men act,

is

is, that it is an Invention of Politicians, to keep Men close to their Promises and Engagements, when all other Ties prov'd ineffectual; and the Christian Religion itself was often found insufficient for that Purpose.

Hor. But the Belief of an over-ruling Power, that will certainly punish Perjury and Injustice, being common to all Religions, what pre-eminence has the Christian over the Rest, as to the Civil Society in Temporals?

Cleo. It shews and insists upon the Necessity of that Belief more amply and more emphatically than any other. Besides, the Strictness of its Morality, and the exemplary Lives of Those who preach'd it, gain'd vast Credit to the mysterious Part of it; and there never had been a Doctrine or Philosophy from which it was so likely to expect, that it would produce Honesty, mutual Love and Faithfulness in the Discharge of all Duties and Engagements as the Christian Religion. The wisest Moralists, before that Time, had laid the greatest Stress on the Reasonableness of their Precepts; and appeal'd to Human Understanding for the Truth of their Opinions. But the Gospel, soaring beyond the Reach of Reason, teaches us many Things, which no

Mor-

Mortal could ever have known, unlefs they
had been reveal'd to him ; and feveral that
muft always remain incomprehenfible to finite
Capacities ; and this is the Reafon, that the
Gofpel preffes and enjoins Nothing with more
Earneftnefs than Faith and Believing.

Hor. But would Men be more fway'd by
Things they believed only, than they would
be by thofe they underftood ?

Cleo. All Human Creatures are fway'd and
wholly govern'd by their Paffions, whatever
fine Notions we may flatter our Selves with;
even thofe who act fuitably to their Knowledge, and ftrictly follow the Dictates of their
Reafon, are not lefs compell'd fo to do by
fome Paffion or other, that fets them to
Work, than others, who bid Defiance and act
contrary to Both, and whom we call Slaves
to their Paffions. To love Virtue for the Beauty of it, and curb one's Appetites becaufe it
is moft reafonable fo to do, are very good
Things in Theory; but whoever underftands
our Nature, and confults the Practice of Human Creatures, would fooner expect from
them, that they fhould abftain from Vice,
for Fear of Punifhment, and do good, in
Hopes of being rewarded for it.

Hor.

Hor. Would you prefer that Goodnefs, built upon Selfifhnefs and Mercenary Principles, to that which proceeds from a Rectitude of Thinking, and a real Love of Virtue and the Reasonablenefs of Mens Actions?

Cleo. We can give no better Proof of our Reasonablenefs, than by judging rightly. When a Man wavers in his Choice, between prefent Enjoyments of Eafe and Pleasure, and the Difcharge of Duties that are troublefome, he weighs what Damage or Benefit will accrue to him upon the Whole, as well from the Neglect as the Obfervance of the Duties that are prefcrib'd to him; and the greater the Punifhment is he fears from the Neglect, and the more tranfcendent the Reward is which he hopes for from the Obfervance, the more reafonably he acts, when he fides with his Duty. To bear with Inconveniencies, Pain, and Sorrow, in Hopes of being eternally Happy, and refufe the Enjoyments of Pleafure, for Fear of being Miferable for ever, are more juftifiable to Reafon, and more confonant to good Senfe, than it is to do it for Nothing.

Hor. But our Divines will tell you, that this Slavifh Fear is unacceptable, and that the

Love

Love of God ought to be the Motive of good Actions.

Cleo. I have Nothing againſt the refin'd Notions of the Love of God, but this is not what I would now ſpeak of. My Deſign was only to prove, that the more firmly Men believe Rewards and Puniſhments from an inviſible Cauſe, and the more this Belief always influences them in all their Actions, the cloſer they'll keep to Juſtice and all Promiſes and Engagements. It is this that was always moſt wanted in the Civil Society; and, before the Coming of *Chriſt,* Nothing had appear'd upon Earth, from which this grand *Deſideratum,* this Bleſſing, might ſo reaſonably be expected as it might from his Doctrine. In the Beginning of Chriſtianity, and whilſt the Goſpel was explain'd without any Regard to Wordly Views, to be a Soldier was thought inconſiſtent with the Profeſſion of a Chriſtian ; but this Strictneſs of the Goſpel-Principles began to be diſapproved of in the Second Century. The Divines of thoſe Days were moſt of them become arrant Prieſts, and ſaw plainly, that a Religion, which would not allow its Votaries to aſſiſt at Courts or Armies, and comply with the vain World, could never
be

be made National; confequently, the Clergy of
it could never acquire any confiderable Power
upon Earth. In Spirituals they were the Succeffors of the Apoftles, but in Temporals
they wanted to fucceed the Pagan Priefts,
whofe Poffeffions they look'd upon with wifh-
ful Eyes ; and Worldly Strength and Authority being abfolutely neceffary to eftablifh
Dominion , it was agreed , that Chriftians
might be Soldiers, and in a juft War fight
with the Enemies of their Country. But Experience foon taught them, that thofe Chriftians, whofe Confciences would fuffer them to
be Soldiers, and to act contrary to the Doctrine of Peace, were not more ftrict Obfervers
of other Duties ; that Pride, Avarice and Revenge ranged among them as they did among
the Heathens, and that many of them were
guilty of Drunkennefs and Incontinence,
Fraud and Injuftice, at the fame Time that
they pretended to great Zeal, and were great
Sticklers for their Religion. This made it
evident, that there could be no Religion fo
ftrict, no Syftem of Morality fo refin'd, nor
Theory fo well meaning, but fome People
might pretend to profefs and follow it, and
yet be loofe Livers, and wicked in their Practice.   *Hor.*

Hor. Those who profess to be of a Theory, which they contradict by their Practice, are, without Doubt, Hypocrites.

Cleo. I have more Charity than to think so. There are real Believers that lead Wicked Lives; and Many stick not at Crimes, which they never would have dared to commit, if the Terrors of the Divine Justice, and the Flames of Hell, had struck their Imagination, and been before them in the same Manner as they really believe they shall be; or if at that Time their Fears had made the same Impression upon them, which they do at others, when the Evil dreaded seems to be near. Things at a Distance, tho' we are sure that they are to come, make little Impression upon us in Comparison with those that are present and immediately before us. This is evident in the Affair of Death: There is No body who does not believe, that he must die, Mr. *Asgil* perhaps excepted; yet it hardly ever employs People's Thoughts, even of Those who are most terribly afraid of it whilst they are in perfect Health, and have every Thing they like. Man is never better pleas'd than when he is employ'd in procuring Ease and Pleasure, in thinking on his own· Worth, and

mend-

mending his Condition upon Earth. Whether This is laid on the Devil or our Attachment to the World, it is plain to me, that it flows from Man's Nature, always to mind to Flatter, Love, and take Delight in himself; and that he cares as little as possible ever to be interrupted in this grand Employment. As every Organ, and every Part of Man, seems to be made and wisely contriv'd for the Functions of this Life only, so his Nature prompts him, not to have any Sollicitude for Things beyond this World. The Care of Self-Preservation we are born with, does not extend it self beyond this Life ; therefore every Creature dreads Death as the Dissolution of its Being, the Term not to be exceeded, the End of All. How various and unreasonable soever our Wishes may be, and how enormous the Multiplicity of our Desires, they terminate in Life, and all the Objects of them are on this Side the Grave.

Hor. Has not a Man Desires beyond the Grave, who buys an Estate, not to be enjoy'd but by his Heirs, and enters into Agreements that shall be binding for a Thousand Years.

Cleo. All the Pleasure and Satisfaction that can arise from the Reflection on our Heirs, is enjoy'd enjoy'd in this Life : And the Benefits and Advantages we wiſh to our Poſterity are of the ſame Nature with thoſe which we would wiſh to our Selves if we were to live; and what we take Care of is, that they ſhall be Rich, keep their Poſſeſſions , and that their Eſtates, Authority and Prerogatives ſhall never diminiſh, but rather encreaſe. We look upon Poſterity as the Effect of which we are the Cauſe, and we reckon our Selves as it were to continue in them.

Hor. But the Ambitious that are in Purſuit of Glory, and ſacrifiſe their Lives to Fame and a laſting Reputation, ſure they have Wiſhes beyond the Grave.

Cleo. Tho' a Man ſhould ſtretch and carry his Ambition to the End of the World, and deſire not to be forgot as long as that ſtood , yet the Pleaſure that ariſes from the Reflection on what ſhall be ſaid of him Thouſands and Thouſands of Years after, can only be enjoy'd in this Life. If a vain Coxcomb, whoſe Memory ſhall die with him, can be but firmly perſuaded, that he ſhall leave an eternal Name, the Reflection may give him as much Pleaſure as the greateſt Hero can receive from reflecting on what ſhall really render

him

him immortal. A Man, who is not regenera-
ted, can have no Notion of another World, or
future Happineſs; therefore his Longing after
it cannot be very ſtrong. Nothing can affect us
forcibly but what ſtrikes the Senſes, or ſuch
Things which we are conſcious of within.
By the Light of Nature only, we are capable
of demonſtrating to our Selves the Neceſſity
of a Firſt Cauſe, a Supreme Being; but the
Exiſtence of a Deity cannot be render'd more
manifeſt to our Reaſon, than his Eſſence is unknown and incomprehenſible to our Under-
ſtanding.

Hor. I don't ſee what you drive at.

Cleo. I am endeavouring to account for the
ſmall Effect and little Force, which Religion,
and the Belief of future Puniſhments, may be
of to mere Man, unaſſiſted with the Divine
Grace. The Practice of nominal Chriſtians is
perpetually claſhing with the Theory they
profeſs. Innumerable Sins are committed in
private, which the Preſence of a Child, or
the moſt inſignificant Perſon, might have hinder'd, by Men who believe God to be omniſ-
cient, and never queſtion'd his Ubiquity.

Hor. But pray, come to the Point, the Origin of Honour.

Cleo.

Cleo. If we confider, that Men are always endeavouring to mend their Condition and render Society more happy as to this World we may eafily conceive, when it was evident that Nothing could be a Check upon Man that was abfent, or at leaft appear'd not to be prefent, how Moralifts and Politicians came to look for Something in Man himfelf, to keep him in Awe. The more they examin'd into Human Nature, the more they muft have been convinced, that Man is fo Selfifh a Creature, that, whilft he is at Liberty, the greateft Part of his Time will always be beftow'd upon himfelf; and that whatever Fear or Reverence he might have for an invifible Caufe, that Thought was often joftled out by others, more nearly relating to himfelf. It is obvious likewife, that he neither loves nor efteems any Thing fo well as he does his own Individual ; and that there is Nothing, which he has fo conftantly before his Eyes, as his own dear Self. It is highly probable, that skilful Rulers, having made thefe Obfervations for fome Time, would be tempted to try if Man could not be made an Object of Reverence to himfelf.

Hor. You have only named Love and Efteem;

teem; they alone cannot produce Reverence by your own Maxim; how could they make a Man afraid of himself?

Cleo. By improving upon his Dread of Shame; and this, I am perfuaded, was the Cafe: For as foon as it was found out, that many vicious, quarrelfome, and undaunted Men, that fear'd neither God nor Devil, were yet often curb'd and vifibly with-held by the Fear of Shame; and likewife that this Fear of Shame might be greatly encreas'd by an artful Education, and be made fuperiour even to that of Death, they had made a Difcovery of a real Tie, that would ferve many noble Purpofes in the Society. This I take to have been the Origin of Honour, the Principle of which has its Foundation in Self-liking; and no Art could ever have fix'd or rais'd it in any Breaft, if that Paffion had not pre-exifted and been predominant there.

Hor. But, how are you fure, that this was the Work of Moralifts and Politicians, as you feem to infinuate?

Cleo. I give thofe Names promifcuoufly to All that, having ftudied Human Nature, have endeavour'd to civilize Men, and render them more and more tractable, either for the Eafe

of

of Governours and Magiſtrates, or elſe for the
Temporal Happineſs of Society in general. I
think of all Inventions of this Sort, the ſame
which told * you of Politeneſs, that they are
the joint Labour of Many. Human Wiſdom is
the Child of Time. It was not the Contrivance of one Man, nor could it have been
the Buſineſs of a few Years, to eſtabliſh a Notion, by which a rational Creature is kept in
Awe for Fear of it Self, and an Idol is ſet up,
that ſhall be its own Worſhiper.

Hor. But I deny, that in the Fear of Shame
we are afraid of our Selves. What we fear,
is the Judgment of others, and the ill Opinion they will juſtly have of us.

Cleo. Examine this thoroughly, and you'll
find, that when we covet Glory, or dread Infamy, it is not the good or bad Opinion of
others that affects us with Joy or Sorrow,
Pleaſure or Pain; but it is the Notion we form
of that Opinion of theirs, and muſt proceed
from the Regard and Value we have for it.
If it was otherwiſe, the moſt Shameleſs Fellow would ſuffer as much in his Mind from
publick Diſgrace and Infamy, as a Man that

* Fable of the Bees, Part. 11. page 132.

va-

values his Reputation. Therefore it is the
Notion we have of Things, our own Thought
and Something within our Selves, that creates
the Fear of Shame: For if I have a Reason,
why I forbear to do a Thing to Day, which
it is impossible should be known before to
Morrow, I must be with-held by Something
that exists already ; for Nothing can act upon
me the Day before it has its Being.

Hor. The Upshot is I find, that Honour is
of the same Origin with Virtue.

Cleo. But the Invention of Honour, as a
Principle, is of a much later Date; and I look
upon it as the greater Atchievement by far.
It was an Improvement in the Art of Flattery, by which the Excellency of our Species
is raised to such a Height, that it becomes the
Object of our own Adoration, and Man is
taught in good Earnest to worship himself.

Hor. But granting you, that both Virtue
and Honour are of Human Contrivance, why
do you look upon the Invention of the One to
be a greater Atchievement than that of the
other?

Cleo. Because the One is more skilfully
adapted to our inward Make. Men are better
paid for their Adherence to Honour, than
they

they are for their Adherence to Virtue : The
First requires lefs Self-denial; and the Rewards
they receive for that Little are not imaginary
but real and palpable. But Experience confirms what I fay : The Invention of Honour
has been far more beneficial to the Civil Society than that of Virtue, and much better
anfwer'd the End for which they were invented. For ever fince the Notion of Honour
has been receiv'd among Chriftians, there have
always been, in the fame Number of People,
Twenty Men of real Honour, to One of real
Virtue. The Reafon is obvious. The Perfuafions to Virtue make no Allowances, nor
have any Allurements that are clafhing with
the Principle of it ; whereas the Men of Pleafure, the Paffionate and the Malicious, may
all in their Turns meet with Opportunities of
indulging their darling Appetites without tref-
paffing againft the Principle of Honour. A
virtuous Man thinks himfelf obliged to obey
the Laws of his Country ; but a Man of Honour acts from a Principle which he is bound
to believe Superiour to all Laws. Do but
confider the Inftinct of Sovereignty that all
Men are born with, and you'll find, that in the
clofeft Attachment to the Principle of Honour
there

there are Enjoyments that are ravishing to Human Nature. A virtuous Man expects no Acknowledgments from others; and if they won't believe him to be virtuous, his Business is not to force them to it; but a Man of Honour has the Liberty openly to proclaim himself to be such, and call to an Account Every body who dares to doubt of it: Nay, such is the inestimable Value he sets upon himself, that he often endeavours to punish with Death the most insignificant Trespass that's committed against him, the least Word, Look, or Motion, if he can find but any far-fetch'd Reason to suspect a Design in it to under-value him; and of this No body is allow'd to be a Judge but himself. The Enjoyments that arise from being virtuous are of that Nicety, that every ordinary Capacity cannot relish them: As, without Doubt, there is a noble Pleasure in forgiving of Injuries, to Speculative Men that have refin'd Notions of Virtue; but it is more Natural to resent them; and in revenging one's self, there is a Pleasure which the meanest Understanding is capable of tasting. It is manifest then, that there are Allurements in the Principle of Honour, to draw in Men of the lowest Capacity, and even the vicious, which Virtue has not.

Hor.

Hor. I can't fee, how a Man can be really virtuous, who is not likewife a Man of Honour. A Perfon may defire to be Honeft, and have an Averfion to Injuftice, but unlefs he has Courage, he will not always dare to be juft, and may on many Occafions be afraid to do his Duty. There is no Dependance to be had on a Coward, who may be bully'd into vicious Actions, and every Moment be frighten'd from his Principle.

Cleo. It never was pretended, that a Man could be Virtuous and a Coward at the fame Time; fince Fortitude is the very Firft of the Four Cardinal Virtues. As much Courage and Intrepidity as you pleafe; but a virtuous Man will never difplay his Valour with Oftentation, where the Laws of God and Men forbid him to make Ufe of it. What I would demonftrate, is, that there are many Allowances, grofs Indulgences to Human Nature in the Principle of Honour, efpecially of modern Honour, that are always exclaim'd againft by the Voice of Virtue, and diametrically oppofite to the Doctrine of *Chrift.*

Hor. Yet the further we look back for thefe Seven or Eight Hundred Years, the more we fhall find Honour and Religion blended together. *Cleo.*

Cleo. When Ignorance, for several Ages, had been successfully encouraged and was designedly introduced to make Way for Credulity, the Simplicity of the Gospel and the Doctrine of *Christ* were turn'd into Gaudy Foppery and vile Superstition. It was then, that the Church of *Rome* began openly to execute her deep-laid Plot for enslaving the Laity. Knowing, that no Power or Authority can be establish'd or long maintain'd upon Earth without real Strength and Force of Arms, she very early coax'd the Soldiery, and made all Men of Valour her Tools by Three Maxims, that, if skilfully follow'd, will never fail of engaging Mankind in our Favour.

Hor. What are those, pray.

Cleo. Indulging Some in their Vices, Humouring Others in their Folly, and Flattering the Pride of All. The various Orders of Knighthood were so many Bulwarks to defend the Temporals of the Church, as well against the Encroachments of her Friends, as the Invasions of her Enemies. It was in the Institutions of these Orders, that Pains were taken by the grand Architects of the Church, to reconcile, in outward Shew, the Principle of Honour with that of the Christian Religion, and

make

make Men ſtupidly believe, that the Height of Pride is not inconſiſtent with the greateſt Humility. In theſe Solemnities the jugling Prieſts reſolved to be kept out no where; had commonly the greateſt Share; continually blending Rites ſeemingly Sacred with the Emblems of vain Glory, which made all of them an eternal Mixture of Pomp and Superſtition.

Hor. I don't believe, that ever Any body ſet thoſe Things in ſuch a Light beſides your Self; but I ſee no Deſign, and the Prieſts gave themſelves a great Deal of Trouble for Nothing.

Cleo. Yet it is certain, that, by this and other Arts, they made themſelves ſure of the moſt dangerous Men; for by this Means the boldeſt and even the moſt wicked became Bigots. The leſs Religion they had, the more they ſtood in Need of the Church; and the farther they went from God, the more cloſely they ſtuck to the Prieſts, whoſe Power over the Laity was then the moſt abſolute and uncontroul'd when the Crimes of Theſe were moſt flagrant and enormous.

Hor. I believe, that among the Men of Honour Many were tainted with Pride and Superſtition at the ſame Time; but there were
Others

others in whom fuperlative Bravery was united with the ftricteft Virtue.

Cleo. All Ages have had Men of Courage,
and all Ages have had Men of Virtue ; but the
Examples of Thofe you fpeak of, in whom
fuperlative Bravery was united with the
ftricteft Virtue, were always extremely fcarce,
and are rarely to be met with, but in Legends
and Romances, the Writers of both which I
take to have been the greateft Enemies to
Truth and fober Senfe the World ever pro-
duc'd.   I don't deny, that by perufing them
Some might have fallen in Love with Courage and Heroifm, others with Chaftity and
Temperance, but the Defign of both was to
ferve the Church of *Rome*, and with won-
derful Stories to gain the Attention of the
Readers, whilft they taught Bigotry, and inu-
red them to believe Impoffibilities. But what
I intended was to point at the People that
had the greateft Hand in reconciling, to outward Appearance, the Principle of Honour
with that of the Chriftian Religion, the Ages
This was done in, and the Reafons for which
it was attempted.   For it is certain, that by
the Maxims I named, the Church made her
felf fure of Thofe who were moft to be fear'd.

Do

Do but caſt your Eyes on the childiſh Farces,
ſome Popes have made great Men the chief
Actors in, and the apiſh Tricks they made
them play, when they found them intoxicated with Pride, and that at the ſame Time
they were Believers without Reſerve. What
Impertinence of tedious Ceremonies have they
made the greateſt Princes ſubmit to, even ſuch
as were noted for being cholerick and impa-
tient! What Abſurdities in Dreſs have they
made them ſwallow for Ornaments and Marks
of Dignity! If in all theſe the Paſſion of Self-
liking had not been highly gratify'd as well as
play'd upon, Men of Senſe could never have
been fond of them, nor could they have been
of that Duration; for many of them are ſtill
remaining even in Proteſtant Countries, where
all the Frauds of Popery have been detected
long ago; and ſuch Veneration is paid to ſome
of them, that it would hardly be ſafe to ridicule them. It is amazing to think, what im-
menſe Multitudes of Badges of Honour have
been invented by Popery, that are all diſtinct
from the Reſt, and yet have Something or
other to ſhew, that they have a Relation to
Chriſtianity. What a vaſt Variety of Shapes,
not reſembling the Original, has the poor
Croſs

Cross been tortur'd into! How differently has
it been placed and represented on the Gar-
ments of Men and Women, from Head to
Foot! How inconsiderable are all other Frauds
that Lay-Rogues now and then have been se-
cretly guilty of, if you compare them to the
bare-fac'd Cheats and impudent Forgeries, with
which the Church of *Rome* has constantly im-
posed upon Mankind in a triumphant Manner! What contemptible Baubles has that
Holy Toy-shop put off in the Face of the Sun
for the richest Merchandize! She has bribed
the most Selfish and penetrating Statesmen,
with empty Sounds, and Titles without Meaning. The most resolute Warriours She has
forced to desist from their Purposes, and do
her dirty Work against their own Interest. I
shall say Nothing of the Holy War; how often the Church has kindled and renew'd it, or
what a Handle She made of it to raise and establish her own Power, and to weaken and
undermine that of the Temporal Princes in
Christendom. The Authority of the Church has
made the greatest Princes and most haughty Sovereigns fall prostrate before, and pay Adoration to the vilest Trumpery, and accept of, as
Presents of inestimable Worth, despicable Trifles

fles, that had no Value at all but what was fet
upon them by the Gigantick Impudence of
the Donors, and the childifh Credulity of the
Receivers. The Church mifled the Vulgar, and
then made Money of their Errors. There is not
an Attribute of God, and hardly a Word in
the Bible, to which fhe gave not fome Turn
or other, to ferve her Worldly Intereft. The
Belief of Witch-craft was the Fore-runner of
Exorcifms; and the Priefts forged Apparitions
to fhew the Power they pretended to, of lay-
ing Spirits, and cafting out Devils. To make
accufed Perfons, fometimes by Ordeal, at others
by fingle Combat, try the Juftice of their
Caufe, were both Arrows out of her Quiver;
and it is from the latter, that the Fafhion of
Duelling took its Rife. But thofe fingle Com-
bats at firft were only fought by Perfons of
great Quality, and on fome confiderable Quarrel, when they ask'd Leave of the Sovereign
to decide the Difference between them by
Feats of Arms; which being obtain'd, Judges
of the Combat were appointed, and the
Champions enter'd the Lift with great Pomp,
and in a very folemn Manner. But as the
Principle of Honour came to be very ufeful,
the Notions of it, by Degrees, were induftri-
 oufly

ously spread among the Multitude, till at last all Swords-men took it in their Heads, that they had a Right to decide their own Quarrels, without asking any Body's Leave. Two Hundred Years ago ———

Hor. Pardon my Rudeness, I cannot stay one Moment. An Affair of Importance requires my Presence. It is an Appointment which I had entirely forgot when I came hither. I am sure I have been staid for this Half Hour.

Cleo. Pray, *Horatio*, make no Apologies. There is no Company I love better than I do yours when you are at Leisure; but ——.

Hor. You don't stir out I know; I shall be back again in Two Hours Time.

Cleo. And I shall be at Home for No body but your Self.

THE

THE
Second Dialogue
BETWEEN
Horatio and *Cleomenes.*

Horatio.

I Believe I am within my Time.

Cleo. By above Ten Minutes.

Hor. When I came back in the Chair, I was thinking how artfully, all this Afternoon, you avoided faying any Thing of Honour, as it relates to the Fair Sex. Their Honour, you know, confifts in their Chaftity, which is a real Virtue in your own Senfe, not to be practis'd without palpable Self-denial. To make a Vow of perpetual Virginity, and to be refolute enough, never to break it, is a Tafk not to be perform'd without the utmoft Mortification to Flefh and Blood, efpecially in hand-

handfome clever Women that feem to be made for Love, as you and I have feen a great many in the Nunneries in *Flanders.* Self-liking or Pride have Nothing to do there ; for the more powerfully that Paffion operates in either Men or Women, the lefs Inclination they'll fhew to be mew'd up in a Cloyfter, where they can have None but their own Sex to converfe with.

Cleo. The Reafon why I faid Nothing of Honour as it relates to the fair Sex, was becaufe we had fpoke of it already in a former Converfation; by the fame Token, that I told you then, that * *the Word Honour, I mean, the Sence of it, was very whimfical, and the Difference in the Signification fo prodigious, according as the Attribute was either applied to a Man, or to a Woman, that neither fhall forfeit their Honour, tho' each fhould be guilty, and openly boaft of what would be the other's greateft Shame.*

Hor. I remember it, and it is true. Gallantry with Women, is no Difcredit to the Men, any more than Want of Courage is a Reproach to the Ladies. But do you think this is an Anfwer to what I faid ?

---

* Fable of the Bees, part 11. page 128.

Cleo.

Cleo. It is an Anſwer to your Charge againſt me of making Uſe of an Artifice, which, I declare to you, never enter'd into my Head. That the Honour of Women in general, is allow'd to conſiſt in their Chaſtity, is very true; the Words themſelves have been made Uſe of as Synonimous even among the Ancients: But this, ſtrictly ſpeaking, ought only to be underſtood of Worldly Women, who act from Political Views, and at beſt from a Principle of Heathen Virtue. But the Women you ſpeak of among the Chriſtians, who, having vow'd a perpetual Virginity, debar themſelves from ſenſual Pleaſures, muſt be ſet on, and animated by a higher Principle than that of Honour. Thoſe who can voluntarily make this Vow in good Humour and Proſperity, as well as Health and Vigour, and keep it with Strictneſs, tho' it is in their Power to break it, have, I own with you, a Taſk to perform, than which Nothing can be more mortifying to Fleſh and Blood. Self-liking or Pride, as you ſay, have Nothing to do there. But where are theſe Women to be found?

Hor. I told you; in the Religious Houſes.

Cleo. I don't believe there is one in a Thouſand that anſwers the Character you gave of
them

them. Moſt Nuns are made whilſt they are
very young, and under the Tuition of others;
and oftner by Compulſion than their own
Choice.

Hor. But there are Women grown, who
take the Veil voluntarily, when they are at
their own Diſpoſal.

Cleo. Not many, who have not ſome ſub-
ſtantial Reaſon or other for it, that has no Relation to Piety or Devotion; ſuch as the Want
of a Portion ſuitable to their Quality; Diſap-
pointments or other Misfortunes in the World.
But to come to the Point. Tnere are but two
Things which, in Celibacy, can make Men or
Women, in Youth and Health, ſtrictly comply with the Rules of Chaſtity; and theſe are
Religion, and the Fear of Shame. Good Chriſtians, that are wholly ſway'd by the Senſe of a
Religious Duty, muſt be ſupernaturally aſſiſted,
and are Proof againſt all Temptations. But
Theſe have always been very ſcarce, and there
are no Numbers of them any where, that one
can readily go to. It would perhaps be an
odious Diſquiſition, whether, among all the
young and middle-aged Women who lead a
Monaſtick Life, and are ſecluded from the
World, there are Any that have, abſtract from
all

all other Motives, Religion enough to secure them from the Frailty of the Flesh, if they had an Opportunity to gratify it to their Liking with Impunity. This is certain, that their Superiors, and Those under whose Care these Nuns are, seem not to entertain that Opinion of the Generality of them. They always keep them lock'd up and barr'd; suffer no Men to converse with them even in Publick, but where there are Grates between them, and not even then within Reach of one another: And tho' hardly a Male Creature of any Kind is allow'd to come near them, yet they are ever suspicious of them, pry into their most Secret Thoughts, and keep constantly a watchful Eye over them.

Hor. Don't you think this must be a great Mortification to young Women?

Cleo. Yes, a forc'd one; but there is no voluntary Self-denial, which was the Thing you spoke of. The Mortification which they feel is like that of Vagabonds in a Work-House: There is no Virtue in the Confinement of either. Both are dissatisfied, without Doubt, but it is because they are not employ'd to their Liking; and what they grieve at, is, that they can't help themselves. But there are Thousands

fands of vain Women, whom no Thoughts of Futurity ever made any Impreffion upon, that lead fingle Lives by Choice, and are at the fame Time careful of their Honour to the greateft Nicety, in the Midft of Temptations , gay fprightly Women, of amorous Complexions, that can deny a paffionate, deferving Lover, whofe Perfon they approve of and admire, when they are alone with him in the dark; and all this from no better Principle than the Fear of Shame, which has its Foundation in Self-liking, and is fo manifeftly derived from that and no other Paffion. You and I are acquainted with Women, that have refufed Honourable Matches with the Men they loved, and with whom they might have been Happy, if they themfelves had been lefs intoxicated with Vanity.

Hor. But when a Woman can marry, and be maintain'd fuitably to her Quality, and fhe refufes a Man upon no other Score, than that his Fortune, or his Eftate, are not equal to her unreafonable Defires, the Paffion fhe acts from is Covetoufnefs.

Cleo. Would you call a Woman covetous, who vifibly takes Delight in Lavifhnefs, and never fhew'd any Value for Money when

She

She had it: One that would not have a Shilling left at the Year's End, tho' she had Fifty Thousand Pounds coming in? All Women confult not what is befitting their Quality: What many of them want is to be maintain'd fuitably to their Merit, their own Worth, which with great Sincerity they think ineftimable, and which confequently no Price can be equal to. The Motive therefore of thefe Women is no other, than what I have call'd it, their Vanity, the undoubted Offspring of Self-liking, a palpable Excefs, an extravagant Degree of the Paffion, that is able to ftifle the loudeft Calls of Nature, and with a high Hand triumphs over all other Appetites and Inclinations. What Sort of Education now do you think the fitteft to furnifh and fill young Ladies with this high Efteem for themfelves and their Reputation, which, whilft it fubfifts and reigns in them, is an ever-watchful and incorruptible Guardian of their Honour? Would you mortify or flatter; leffen or increafe in them the Paffion of Self-liking, in order to preferve their Chaftity? In fhort, which of the Two is it, you would ftir up and cultivate in them if you could, Humility or Pride?

Hor

Hor. I fhould not try to make them Humble, I own : And now I remember, that in our Third Converfation, fpeaking of raifing the Principle of Honour in both Sexes, you gave fome plaufible Reafons why * Pride fhould be more encourag'd in Women than in Men. So much for the Ladies. I fhall now be glad to hear what you have to add further concerning Honour, as it relates to Men only, and requires Courage. When I took the Freedom to interupt you, you was faying Something of Two Hundred Years ago.

Cleo. I was then going to put you in Mind, that Two Hundred Years ago and upward, as all Gentlemen were train'd up to Arms, the Notions of Honour were of great Ufe to them; and it was manifeft, that never any Thing had been invented before, that was half fo effectual to create artificial Courage among Military Men. For which Reafon it was the Intereft of all Politicians, among the Clergy, as well as the Laity, to cultivate thefe Notions of Honour with the utmoft Care, and leave no Stone unturn'd to make Every body believe the Exiftence and Reality of fuch a Principle;

---

* Fable of the Bees part 11. p. 126.

not among Mechanicks, or any of the Vulgar, but in Perfons of high Birth, Knights, and others of Heroick Spirit and exalted Nature. I can eafily imagine, how, in a credulous, igno-rant Age, this might be fwallow'd and general-ly receiv'd for Truth ; nor is it more difficult to conceive, how illiterate Men and rude Warriours, altogether unacquainted with Hu-man Nature, fhould be fo far impofed upon by fuch Affertions, as to be fully perfuaded, that they were really poffefs'd of; and actually ani-mated by fuch a Principle, conftantly afcri-bing to the Force and Influence of it every Effort and Suggeftion they felt from the Paf-fion of Self-liking. The Idol it felf was fine-ly drefs'd up, made a beautiful Figure, and the Worfhip of it feem'd to require Nothing, that was not highly commendable and moft beneficial to Society. Thofe who pretended to pay their Adoration to it, and to be true Vo-taries of Honour, had a hard Tafk to perform. They were to be Brave and yet Courteous, Juft, Loyal, and the Protectors of Innocence, againft Malice and Oppreffion. They were to be the profefs'd Guardians of the Fair; and chafte, as well as profound Admirers of the Sex : But above all, they were to be Stanch to

the

the Church, implicite Believers, zealous Champions of the Chriftian Faith, and implacable Enemies to all Infidels and Hereticks.

Hor. I believe, that between Two and Three Hundred Years ago, Bigotry was at the greateft Height.

Cleo. The Church of *Rome* had, long before that Time, gain'd fuch an Afcendant over the Laity, that Men of the higheft Quality ftood in Awe of the leaft Parifh-Prieft. This made Superftition fafhionable; and the moft refolute Heroes were not afhamed to pay a blind Veneration to every Thing which the Clergy was pleafed to call Sacred. Men had an entire Confidence in the Pope's Power; his bleffing of Swords, Armours, Colours and Standards; and No body doubted of the Influence, which Saints and Angels had upon Earth, the miraculous Virtue of Relicks, the Reality of Witches and Enchantments, the Black Art, or that Men might be made invulnerable.

Hor. But the Ignorance of thofe Days notwithftanding, you believe, that there were Men of that ftrict Honour, you have been fpeaking of.

Cleo. Men of Honour, I told you, were required and fuppofed to be poffefs'd of thofe

Qua-

Qualities ; and I believe, that several endeavour'd to be, and some actually were such, as
far as Human Frailty would let them ; but I
believe likewise, that there were others, who
gain'd the Title, by their Undauntedness only,
and had but a small Stock of any other Virtue
besides; and that the Number of these was
always far the greatest. Courage and Intrepidity always were, and ever will be the grand
Characteristick of a Man of Honour : It is this
Part of the Character only, which it is always
in our Power to demonstrate. The best Friend
a King has, may want an Opportunity to
shew his Loyalty : So a Man may be just and
chaste, and yet not be able to convince the
World that he is so ; but he may pick a **Quar-**
rel, and shew, that he dares to Fight when he
pleases, especially if he converses with Men of
the Sword. Where the Principle of Honour
was in high Esteem, Vanity and Impatience
must have always prompted the most proud
and forward to seek after Opportunities of Sig-
nalizing themselves, in order to be stiled Men
of Honour. This would naturally occasion
Quarrelling and Fighting, as it did and had
frequently done before the Time I speak of.
As Duelling was made a Fashion, the Point of
Ho-

Honour became, of Courfe, a common Topick of Difcourfe among the beft bred Men:
By this Means the Rules for Quarrelling and
Punctilio in Behaviour, which at firft were
very uncertain and precarious, came to be
better underftood, and refin'd upon from Time
to Time, till, in the Beginning of the laft Century, the Senfe of Honour was arrived to
fuch a Degree of Nicety all over *Europe*, efpecially in *France*, that barely looking upon
a Man was often taken for an Affront. The
Cuftom of Duelling, by this, was become fo
univerfal in that Kingdom, that the Judges
themfelves thought it difhonourable to refufe
a Challenge. *Henry* IVth. feeing the beft Blood
of *France* fo often facrific'd to this Idol, endeavour'd to put a Stop to it, but was not able;
and the feveral Edicts made in 1602 and 1609
were fruitlefs. The Refolutions of Parliament
likewife, made in the Reign of *Lewis* XIIIth.
were as ineffectual: The Firft Check that
was given to Duelling, was in the Minority
of *Lewis* XIVth, and from the Method by
which it was prevented at laft, it is evident,
that Honour is an Idol, by Human Contrivance, rais'd on the Bafis of Human Pride.

Hor·

Hor. The Method by which a Stop was put to it, was ſtrictly to puniſh and never to pardon Any that either ſent or accepted of Challenges, whether they fought or not.

Cleo. This was not truſted to only. An Edict was publiſh'd in the Year 1651, by which Courts of Honour were erected throughout the Kingdom, with Gentlemen Commiſſioners in every Bailiwick, that were to have Advice of, and immediately to interpoſe in all Differences that might ariſe between Gentlemen. The Difficulty they labour'd under was, that they would aboliſh the Cuſtom of Duelling without parting with the Notions of Honour; deſtroying of which muſt have been certain Ruin to a warlike Nation, that once had received them ; and therefore they never deſign'd, that the Worſhip of the Idol ſhould ceaſe, but they only try'd, whether it was not to be ſatisfied with leſs valuable Victims, and other Sacrifices beſides human Blood. In the Year 1653, *Lewis* XIV. ſet forth another Declaration againſt Duels; in which having made ſome Additions to his former Edict, he commands the Marſhals of *France* to draw up a Regulation touching the Satisfactions and Reparations of Honour, which they ſhould
think

think neceſſary for the ſeveral Sorts of Offences. This Order was immediately obey'd, and
nineteen Articles were drawn up and publiſh'd
accordingly. In theſe, calling a Man Fool,
Coward, or the Like, was puniſh'd with a
Month's Impriſonment ; and after being relea-
ſed, the Offender was to declare to the Party
ſo offended, that he had wrongfully and im-
pertinently injur'd him by outragious Words,
which he own'd to be falſe, and aſk'd him to
forgive. Giving one the Lie, or threatning to
beat him, was two Month's Impriſonment, and
the Submiſſion to be made afterwards yet more
humble than the foregoing. For Blows, as
ſtriking with the Hand, and other Injuries of
the ſame Nature, the Offender was to lye in
Priſon Six Months, unleſs, at the Requeſt of
the offended, half of that Time was chang'd
into a pecuniary Mulⅽt, that might not be under Fifteen Hundred Livres, to be paid before
he was ſet at Liberty, for the Uſe of the nea-
reſt Hoſpital to the Abode of the offended ; after which, the Offender was to ſubmit to the
ſame Blows from the offended, and to declare
by Word of Mouth, and in Writing, that he
had ſtruck him in a Brutiſh Manner, and beg'd
him to pardon and forget that Offence.

Hor.

Hor. What Mortal could fubmit to fuch Condefcenfions?

Cleo. For Caning, or Blows given with a Stick, the Punifhment was ftill more fevere; and the Offender was to beg pardon upon his Knees.

Hor. I fhould have no great Opinion of a Man's Honour, who would not chufe to Die rather than comply with fuch Demands.

Cleo. Several thought as you do, and were hang'd for their Pains. But what Need a Man come to thofe Extremes, when he could have Satisfaction for any real Offence that might provoke him? For the Articles took Notice of, and made ample Provifions againft all Manner of Injuries, from the moft trifling Offences to the higheft Outrages, and were very fevere againft all thofe that fhould refufe to fubmit to the Penalties impofed. The Marfhals of *France* remain'd the Supreme Judges in all thefe Matters; and under them acted the Governours and Lieutenants General of Provinces, in whofe Abfence the Gentlemen Commiffioners in every Bailiwick, having Power to call the Officers of Juftice to their Affiftance, were to take all provifional Care imaginable; fo that no Lawyers or Mechanicks
had

had a Hand in compofing any Differences concerning the Point of Honour.

Hor. All thefe Things, we'll fay, are wifely
contriv'd ; but in complaining firft there is a
Meannefs, which a Man of Honour cannot
ftoop to.

Cleo. That the Inftinct of Sovereignty will
always bid Men revenge their own Wrongs,
and do Juftice to themfelves, is certain.   But
I wanted to fhew you the Equivalent, that
wife Men fubftituted in the Room of Dueling, and which Men of unqueftion'd Honour
took up with.   The Scheme was contrived
by Men of tried Valour, whofe Example is
always of great Weight : Befides, from the
Nature of the Remedies that were applied
to the Evil, it muft always follow, that thofe
who had given the greateft Proofs of their
Courage, would be the moft ready to fubfcribe
to thofe Articles.

Hor. In our laft Converfation but one you
told me, that * all Laws pointed at, and tally'd
with fome Frailty or Paffion in our Nature ;
pray, what is it that thefe Laws of Honour
tally with ?

Cleo. It is felf-evident, that they point at Self-

---

* Fable of the Bees, part II. page 318.

lik-

liking and the Inftinct of Sovereignty. But
what is fingular in thefe Laws is, that in their
Operation they are the reverfe of all others.

Hor. I don't underftand you.

Cleo. All other Precepts and Command-
ments are vifibly labouring to reftrain the Paffions, and cure the Imperfections of our Nature; but thefe Regulations of Honour are
endeavouring to prevent Mifchief, by foothing
and flattering the Frailties they point at. In
Offences againft a Man's Honour, Pardon is
not afk'd of God or the King, but of him who
receiv'd the Affront. It is he, therefore, whom
all the Addrefs and Homage are paid to: He
is the Idol that is kneel'd to, and the only Sovereign that can forgive the Trefpaffes committed againft himfelf. The Punifhment of
the firft Aggreffor, you fee, is altogether a
Compliment to the Perfon offended, whofe
Wrath the Law is fo far from blaming, that
it juftifies it, and gives him an Opportunity
of indulging it by the Indignity it puts upon
the Offender. The real Mifchief is not apprehended from the Offender, but the Perfon
offended; and therefore it is him, whom the
Law coaxes and wheedles into good Humour,
by offering him a Reparation that fhall be
equal-

equally honourable with what he would chuſe, tho' leſs prejudicial to the Society. What the Law promiſes is a Tribute to the ſame Paſſion which he wants to gratify, a Sacrifice to the Idol which he himſelf adores. Should Any one perſonate theſe Laws, and, re-preſenting the Sentiments of thoſe who made them, ſpeak to a Man of Honour, who had receiv'd an Affront, an Officer of the Guards, we'll ſay, who had been call'd Fool by his Equal, the Purport of the Diſcourſe would be this: You are very much in the Right, Sir, to be highly incenſed againſt the Man who da-red to call you Fool, you that are a Man of Honour, to whom, as ſuch, the whole World ought to pay the higheſt Eſteem. You have not only an undoubted Right to do your Self Juſtice, and revenge the Affront that has been given you; but there is likewiſe ſuch a Neceſ-ſity of your reſenting it, that if you could tame-ly put up the Injury you have receiv'd, and neg-lect demanding Satisfaction, you would deſerve to be branded with Ignominy, and all Men of Honour would juſtly refuſe ever to converſe with you for the future. But the Perſon, whom you have this Affair with, being likewiſe a Man of Honour, it is greatly to be fear'd, that upon

your

your demanding Satisfaction of him, a Battle
will enfue, which, between two Perfons who
value their Honours a Thoufand Times more
than their Lives, will probably be fatal to one,
if not to both; you are therefore earneftly defired by the King himfelf, that for his Sake you
would make fome Alteration in the Manner of
taking that Satisfaction which you ought to
receive; and the Marfhals of *France* have
not only given it under their Hands, that the
Equivalents, which they have propofed for
Fighting, will be as entire a Reparation to
your Honour as can be obtain'd by Arms;
but moreover they have promifed and engaged their Honours, that in Cafes of Affronts
they will take up and content themfelves with
the fame Equivalents, and on all Occafions
fubmit to the fame Regulations, which you
are now defired to follow. And that it may
appear, how highly reafonable this Requeft is,
you are likewife defired to take the following
Remonftrance into your Confideration: That
the Valour and Steadinefs of Men of Honour
are the grand Support of all States and Kingdoms, is a Truth not to be denied; and that
not only the Peace and Tranquility, and all
the Bleffings we enjoy, but likewife the King's
Crown

Crown and Safety would be precarious without them, is as unqueſtionable. For this Reaſon all wiſe Princes, Magiſtrates and Governours, will ever take all imaginable Care, on the one Hand, to cultivate and encourage the moſt noble Principle of Honour, and, on the other, to encreaſe the Numbers of the worthy Profeſſors of it, by favouring and on all Occaſions ſhewing them the moſt tender Affection, as well as higheſt Eſteem. It is eaſy then to be imagin'd, that a Monarch, who loves his People, and has the Intereſt of his Nation at Heart, muſt be ſenſibly afflicted to ſee it become a common Practice for ſuch valuable Men to deſtroy one another, and behold that Bravery and Spirit, which ſhould only be made Uſe of againſt the Enemies of the Country, hourly employ'd and laviſh'd away in private Quarrels, that can have no other Tendency than the weakning of the Kingdom, and which, if ſuffer'd to go on, muſt compleat its Ruin.

Hor. You make theſe Laws ſpeak very notably.

Cleo. I have ſaid Nothing but what is certainly imply'd in them. Every Man in *France* knew, that the chief Motive of all thoſe Edicts againſt Duelling, was the Loſs of the brave Men,

Men that was fuftain'd by that Cuftom. The Sinfulnefs of it was the leaft Confideration.

Hor. There, I believe, you wrong them, for I have feen fome of thefe Edicts, where Dueling is call'd an Antichriftian Practice, which God was highly offended at.

Cleo. In wording of the Edicts, indeed, fome fuch Thing was put in for Form's Sake ; but the Regulations themfelves, by which the Men of Honour were to walk, were openly Antichriftian ; and in fome Cafes, inftead of Teaching Men to forgive thofe that had trefpas'd againft them, they obliged and forced the Offended to fhew their Refentment, tho' they would rather not, and defired to be excufed.

Hor. Where the Affront was very heinous, I know what you fay is true. But you fet thefe Things in a ftrange Light. I can make the fame Gloffes upon our Laws, which oblige me to profecute a Man that has robb'd me, if I can catch him, whether I will or not ; and he fhall be hang'd, tho' I forgive him the Injury, and even would beg his Life.

Cleo. There is a vaft Difference between the two Cafes, a Robbery, and an Affront: No body hinders you from forgiving a Man that robb'd you ; but notwithftanding your pardon-

doning him, he is punifh'd for acting againft
the Laws; therefore his Offence is againft the
King, who is the Guardian and Superinten-
dant of them. And No body but the King
can pardon the Trefpaffes that are committed
againft his Crown and Dignity. Whoever robs
you, muft be hang'd, becaufe he robb'd, not
becaufe he robb'd YOU in particular: Tho'
you are bound to profecute him for Robbing
you, yet the Injury is reckon'd as done to the
Publick; and you become a Criminal your
Self, if you connive at his Efcape, tho' he re-
ftor'd to you what he had robb'd you of. But in
the Cafe of an Affront the Injury is reckon'd to
be done to him only who receiv'd it. His Anger, as I faid before, is thought to be juft,
and his Refentment reafonable, till an ample
Satisfaction be made him; therefore it is He
who is to be appeas'd, and He only who is to
be applied to. The Laws that were compiled
by the Marfhals of *France*, don't pretend to
mend the Heart, and lay no greater Reftraint
on the Spirit of Revenge, than Matrimony
does on the Defire of Procreation; on the Contrary, they flatter the Frailty, and are admi-
niftring to the Haughtinefs of the offended :
They are fo far from denying him his Demands

mands, or refusing to give him Satisfaction
for the Affront, that they appoint it by Authority ; in the ordering of which they make
such ample Provisions for the Gratification of
his Pride, as no reasonable Man could ever
think of without blushing. The only Thing
they oblige him to is, that he shall take the
Satisfaction in such a Manner, as shall be most
safe to himself, and least detrimental to the
Publick. Now if you will consider first, that
those who made these Regulations were Men
of undoubted Honour, who hourly feeling the
Force of it within themselves, were perfectly well acquainted with the Principle which
it is built upon ; and secondly, that the profound Humility of the Offender, and his asking Pardon of the offended, are two main
Points in the repairing of Honour, necessary
postulata, without which those knowing Judges thought it impossible, that an Affront could
be forgiven : If, I say, you'll consider these
two Things, you'll see plainly, what Passion
in Human Nature it is, which those Laws of
Honour tally'd with, and likewise that it is
true, what I have asserted of them, that instead
of reproving, curbing, or diminishing the
Frailty that is offensive, which seems to be
the

the Intention of all other Laws, their Aim is to prevent Mischief and do Service to the Civil Society, by approving of, cherishing, and indulging that very Passion, from which the Evil they would prevent can only proceed.

Hor. You think those Regulations were effectual, and yet you seem to dislike them.

Cleo. I dislike them because they are destructive to Religion; and if a Minister of the Gospel was to dissuade and deter Men from Duelling, he would do it in quite another Manner. By a Minister of the Gospel I don't mean a Philosophizing Divine, or a polite Preacher, but a sincere Follower of the Apostles, a downright Christian. He would, in the First Place, insist upon it, that Forgiving of Injuries was a Christian Duty never to be dispens'd with; because it is made the Condition on which we are taught to beg Pardon for our own Offences. In the Second, he would demonstrate, that no Man is ever to revenge himself, how highly and how atrociously soever he might have been injured. If ever he heard of a Man's sending a Challenge for having been call'd Fool, or other verbal Injuries, he would reprove his Frowardness and Want of Temper, for resenting such Trifles as the Laws of his

Coun-

Country thought it not worthy to take Notice of. He would appeal to his Reafon, and afk him, whether he could think, that the Affront he complain'd of, was a fufficient Caufe. to take away a Man's Life. He would reprefent to him the Heinoufnefs of Murder, God's exprefs Command againft it ; his Juftice, his Wrath, his Vengeance when provok'd. But if all thefe could not divert the Dueller from his Purpofe, he would attack his ftubborn Heart in its inmoft Receffes, and forget Nothing of what I told you on the Subject in our Second and Third Converfation. He would recommend to him the Fable of the *Bees*, and, like that, he'd diffect and lay open to him the Principle of Honour, and fhew him, how diametrically oppofite the Worfhip of that Idol was to the Chriftian Religion; the Firft confifting in openly cherifhing and feeding that very Frailty in our Nature, which the latter ftrictly commands us with all our Might to conquer and deftroy. Having convinced him of the fubftantial Difference and Contrariety between thefe Two Principles, he would difplay to him, on the one Hand, the Vanity of Earthly Glory, and the Folly of Covering the Applaufe of a SinfulWorld; and, on the other,

the

the Certainty of a Future State, and the Tranf-
cendency of everlafting Happinefs over every
Thing that is perifhable. From fuch Remon-
ftrances as thefe the good, pious Man would take
an Opportunity of exhorting him to a Chriftian Self-denial, and the Practice of real Virtue,
and he would earneftly endeavour to make him
fenfible of the Peace of Confcience and folid
Comforts that are to be found in Meeknefs
and Humility, Patience, and an entire Refignation to the Will of God.

Hor. How long, pray, do you intend to
go on with this Cant?

Cleo. If I am to perfonate a Chriftian Divine, who is a fincere Believer, you muft give
me Leave to fpeak his Language.

Hor. But if a Man had really fuch an Affair
upon his Hands, and he knew the Perfon, he
had to do with, to be a refolute Man that underftood the Sword, do you think he would
have Patience or be at Leifure to hearken to all
that puritanical Stuff, which you have been
heaping together? Do you think (for that is
the Point) it would have any Influeuce over
his Actions?

Cleo. If he believ'd the Gofpel, and confe-
qnently future Rewards and Punifhments, and
he

he likewife acted confiftently with what he believ'd, it would put an entire Stop to all, and it would certainly hinder him from fending or accepting of Challenges, or ever engaging in any Thing relating to a Duel.

Hor. Pray now, among all the Gentlemen of your Acquaintance, and fuch as you your Self fhould care to converfe with, how many are there, do you think, on whom the Thoughts of Religion would have that Effect?

Cleo. A great many, I hope.

Hor. You can hardly forbear laughing, I fee, when you fay it; and I am fure, you your Self would have no Value for a Man whom you fhould fee tamely put up a grofs Affront: Nay, I have feen and heard Parfons and Bifhops themfelves laugh at, and fpeak with Contempt of pretended Gentlemen, that had fuffer'd themfelves to be ill treated without refenting it.

Cleo. What you fay of my felf, I own to be true; and I believe the fame of others, Clergymen as well as Laymen. But the Reafon why Men, who bear Affronts with Patience, are fo generally defpifed is, becaufe Every body imagines, that their Forbearance does not proceed from a Motive of Religion, but a Principle of Cowardice. What chiefly induces

duces us to believe this, is the Knowledge we have of our selves: We are conscious within of the little Power which Christianity has over our Hearts, and the small Influence it has over our Actions. Finding our own Incapacity of subduing strong Passions, but by the Help of others that are more violent, we judge of others in the same Manner : And therefore when we see a vain, worldly Man gain such a Conquest over his known and well establish'd Pride, we presently suspect it to be a Sacrifice which he makes to his Fear; not the Fear of God, or Punishment in another World, but the Fear of Death, the strongest Passion in our Nature, the Fear that his Adversary, the Man who has affronted him, will kill him, if he fights him. What confirms us in this O-pinion is, that Poltrons shew no greater Piety or Devotion than other People, but live as voluptuously and indulge their Pleasures as much, at least, as any other of the *beau monde.* Whereas a good Christian is all of a Piece; his Life is uniform ; and whoever should scruple to send or to accept of a Challenge for the Love of God, or but from a Fear of his Vengeance, depend upon it, he would have that same Fear before his Eyes on other Occasions

likewise

likewife: And it is impoffible that a Religious
Principle, which is once of that Force, that
it can make a Man chufe to be defpis'd by the
World, rather than he would offend God,
fhould not only not be confpicuous throughout
his Behaviour, but likewife never influences
the Reft of his Actions at any other Time.

Hor. From all this it is very plain, that there
are very few fincere Chriftians.

Cleo. I don't think fo, as to Faith and Theory ; and I am perfuaded, that there are great
Numbers in all Chriftian Countries, who fincerely believe the Bible to be the Word of
God, and the old as well as new Teftament
to be a Revelation from Heaven: But as to
Works and Practice I am of your Opinion; and
I not only believe, that there are very few
fincere and real Chriftians in their Lives and
Converfation, for that is a difficult Task ; but
I believe likewife, that there are very Few who
are fincere in endeavouring to be fo, or even
in defiring to be real Chriftians. But this is
no Argument againft Chriftianity, or the Rea-
fonablenefs of its Doctrine.

Hor. I don't fay it is. But as the Principle
of Honour, whatever Origin it had, teaches
Men to be juft in all their Dealings, and true

to their Engagements, and there are confiderable Numbers in every civiliz'd Nation, who really take Delight in this Principle, and in all their Actions are fway'd and govern'd by it, muft you not allow, that fuch a Principle, let it be owing to Education, to Flattery, to Pride, or what you pleafe, is more ufeful to Society than the beft Doctrine in the World, which None can live up to, and but Few endeavour to follow?

Cleo. Tho' thofe who are deem'd to be Men of Honour, are far from being all really virtuous, yet I can't difprove, that the Principle of Honour, fuch as it is, does not fully as much Good to Society as Chriftianity, as it is practifed; I fay, to Society, and only in refpect to Temporals; but it is altogether deftructive as to another World: And as the greateft Happinefs upon Earth to a good Chriftian, is a firm Belief, and well grounded Hope, that he fhall be Happy in Heaven, fo a Man who believes the Gofpel, and pretends to value everlafting Happinefs beyond any Thing of fhorter Duration, muft act inconfiftently with himfelf, unlefs he adheres to the Precepts of Chriftianity, and at the fame Time explodes the Principle of Honour, which is the very Reverfe of it.

Hor.

Hor. I own, that in the Light you have put them, they seem to be, as you say, diametrically opposite.

Cleo. You see, that those who act from a Principle of Religion, fairly attack the Heart, and would abolish Duelling and all other Mischief, by restraining, conquering, and destroying of Pride, Anger, and the Spirit of Revenge; but these Passions are so necessary to Society for the Advancement of Dominion and worldly Glory, that the Great and Ambitious could not do without them in a Warlike Nation. Those who compiled in *France* the Regulations we have been speaking of, were well aware of this: They judged from what they felt within, and knew full well, that take away Pride, and you spoil the Soldier; for it is as impossible to strip a Man of that Passion, and preserve in him his Principle of Honour, as you can leave him his Bed after you have taken away the Feathers. A peaceful Disposition and Humility are not Qualities more promising in the Day of Battle, than a contrite Heart and broken Spirit are Preparatives for Fighting. In these Regulations, so often mention'd, it is plainly to be seen, what Pains and Care were taken, not to arraign, or lay the least

Blame

Blame upon the Principle of Honour, tho' the Kingdom groan'd under a Calamity which vifibly arofe from, and could be the Effect of no other Caufe than that very Principle.

Hor. All the Fault, in my Opinion, ought to be laid on the Tyranny of Cuftom ; and therefore the Marfhals of *France* were in the Right not to depreciate or run the leaft Rifque of deftroying or leffening the Principle of Honour, which, I am confident, has been a greater Tie upon Men than any Religion whatever

Cleo. It is impoffible that there fhould be a greater Tie, a ftronger Barrier againft Injuftice than the Chriftian Religion, where it is fincerely believ'd, and Men live up to that Belief. But if you mean, that the Number of Men, who have ftuck to the Principle of Honour, and ftrictly follow'd the Dictates of it, has been greater than that of Chriftians, who, with equal Strictnefs, have obey'd the Precepts of the Gofpel ; if, I fay, you mean this, I don't know how to contradict you. But I thought, that I had given you a very good Reafon for that, when I fhew'd you, that in the Notions of Honour there are many Allurements to draw-in vain worldly Men, which the Chriftian Religion has not ; and that the Severity

of

of this is more mortifying and difagreable to Human Nature, than the Self-denial which is required in the other. There are other Reafons befides, which I have likewife hinted at more than once. A Man may believe the Torments of Hell, and ftand in great Dread of them, whilft they are the Object of his ferious Reflection ; but he does not always think of them, nor will they always make the fame Impreffion upon him, when he does. But in worfhiping Honour, a Man adores himfelf, which is ever dear to him, never abfent, never out of Sight. A Man is eafily induced to reverence what he loves fo entirely.

Hor. The Fear of Shame cannot reftrain Men in Things that are done in Secret, and can never be known. Men of Honour are true to their Truft, where it is impoffible they fhould be difcover'd.

Cleo. That is not univerfally true; tho' without doubt, there are many fuch. The grand Characteriftick of a Man of Honour, at leaft of Modern Honour, is, that he takes no Affront without refenting it, and dares fight Any body without Exception ; and fuch there are that have not common Honefty, and are noted Sharpers. Befides, by Education and converfing

fing conftantly with Men of Honour, and Some of real Honour and Probity, Perfons may contract a ftrong Averfion to every Thing that is difhonourable. The moft effectual Method to breed Men of Honour, is to infpire them with lofty and romantick Sentiments concerning the Excellency of their Nature, and the fuperlative Merit there is in being a Man of Honour. The higher you can raife a Man's Pride, the more refin'd you may render his Notions of Honour.

Hor. The Subftance of this you have faid twenty Times ; but I don't underftand your adoring of one's felf.

Cleo. I'll endeavour to explain it to you. I am acquainted with Men of Honour, who feem to have a very flender Belief, if any, of future Rewards and Punifhments, and whom yet I believe to be very juft Men. Of thefe there are feveral, whom I could entirely confide in, and whofe Words I would much rather take in Bufinefs of Moment than any Bifhop's, whom I knew Nothing of. What is it that keeps thefe Men in Awe ? What keeps them true to their Word, and fteady to their Engagements, tho' they fhould be Lofers by it ?

Hor.

Hor. I don't know any Thing but the Principle of Honour, that is deeply rooted in them.

Cleo. Still the Thing, whatever it be, which a Man loves, fears, esteems, and consequently reverences, is not without, but within himself. The Object then of Reverence, and the Worshiper, who pays it, meeting and remaining in the same Person, may not such a Person be justly said to adore himself: Nay, it seems to be the common Opinion, that this is true; for unless some Sort of Divinity was supposed to reside in Men of Honour, their affirming and denying Things upon that Principle could never be thought an Equivalent for an Oath, as to Some it is allow'd to be. Pray, when a Man asserts a Thing upon his Honour, is it not a Kind of Swearing by himself, as others do by God? If it was not so, and there was supposed to be the least Danger, that Men, endued with the Principle of Honour, could deceive or prevaricate, I would fain know, why it should be binding and acquiesc'd in.

Hor. You may say the same of the Quakers; and that there must be supposed to be some Divinity in them, that their solemn Affirmation should be thought equivalent to an Oath. *Cleo.*

Cleo. That's quite another Thing. The Quakers take all Oaths whatever, whether they are made before a Magiftrate or otherwife, to be finful, and for that Reafon they refufe to Swear at all. But as it is their avow'd Opinion, that a wilful notorious Lie is not lefs Criminal in the Sight of Heaven than we take Perjury to be, it is evident, that in giving their Teftimony, they ftake their Salvation equally with other People that make Oath. Whereas thofe who, with us, are credited upon their Honour, have no fuch Scruples, and make Oath themfelves on other Occafions: The Reafon therefore why they don't try Criminals and pronounce their Judgment upon Oath, as other Judges and Juries do, is not, that they think appealing to God or Swearing by his Name to be Sinful, which is the Cafe of the Quakers; but becaufe they are fuppofed to be altogether as credible without it, as if they did. And if there was not fome Adoration, fome Worfhip, which Men of Honour pay to themfelves, the Principle they act from could not have produced the vifible Effects it has in fo many different Nations.

Hor. You have faid feveral Things which I cannot difprove, and fome of them, I own, are

are probable enough ; but you are like to
leave me as you found me. The Principle
of Honour has loft no Ground in my Efteem ;
and I fhall continue to act from it as I did before. But fince you imagine to have fo plainly proved, that we are Idols to our Selves, and
that Honour is diametrically oppofite to Chriftianity, I wonder you don't call it the Beaft
in the *Apocalypfe,* and fay, that it is the
Whore of *Babylon.* This would be a notable
Conceit, and fuit Papifts as well as Proteftants;
nay, I fancy, that the Colour of the Whore,
and her Thirft after Blood, might be better
accounted for from Duelling, than any other
Way that has been tried yet.

Cleo. The Revelations of St. *John* are above
my Comprehenfion; and I fhall never laugh at
Myfteries for not underftanding them.

Hor. What you fay of Myfteries, I think,
ought to be more juftly applied to the Principle of Honour, which we do underftand; for
whatever it may be derived from, the Advantages the Civil Society receives from it, both
in Peace and War, are fo many and fo manifeft, that the Ufefulnefs of it ought to exempt
and preferve it from being ridicul'd. I hate to
hear a Man talk of its being more or lefs por-
table,

table, the melting of it over again, and reducing it to a new Standard.

Cleo. I know, you diſlike this in the Fable of the *Bees*; but if you'll examine into what you have read there, you'll find, that my Friend has ridicul'd Nothing but what deſerves it. There is certainly a great Difference between the Men of Honour in former Ages and many of thoſe, who now-a-days aſſume the Title. A Man in whom Juſtice, Integrity, Temperance and Chaſtity are join'd with Fortitude, is worthy of the higheſt Eſteem ; but that a debauch'd Fellow, who runs in every Tradesman's Debt, and thinks himſelf not obliged to pay any Thing but what is borrow'd or loſt at Play, ſhould claim the ſame Regard from us, for no other Reaſon than becauſe he dares to Fight, is very unreaſonable.

Hor. But is he ſerious, when he ſpeaks of the Men of ancient Honour, of whom he thinks *Don Quixot* to have been the laſt ?

Cleo. When the Romance-Writers had carried the Prowefs and Atchievements of their Heroes to an incredible Pitch, was it not ridiculous to ſee Men in their Senſes, not only believe thoſe Extravagancies in good Earneſt, but likewiſe endeavour to imitate thoſe fabulous

lous Exploits, and set about copying after those imaginary Patterns? For it was that which *Cervantes* exposed in *Don Quixot*.

Hor. In the Fifteenth and Sixteenth Century, the *Spaniards* were the best Soldiers in the World; they shew'd themselves on many Emergencies to be a grave and wise Nation, and had many real Patterns of strict Honour and great Virtue among them. Things are as often over-done in Satyrs as they are in Panegyricks; and the Likeness of a *Caricatura* is no more to be trusted to than that of the most flattering Pencil.

Cleo. I shall always bear the highest Esteem for Men of strict Honour and real Virtue, and will never ridicule what is approved of by Custom, and the Consent of several Ages has render'd valuable; but no Title or Dignity, no Name or Distinction can be so honourable, or so eminent, that a serious Enquirer may not have Leave to trace it to the Bottom. I have acknowledged, that the Word Honour, in its first and genuine Sense, is as ancient as the oldest Language in the World. As to my Conjecture concerning the same Word, as it signifies a Principle which Men act from, I leave it entirely to your Judgment: But whatever
the

the Origin may be of either, it is certain, that whatever the Words Honour and Honourable are join'd with, added or applied to, there is a plain Defign in them of pleafing and gratifying thofe it concerns, on Account of the Paffion of Self-liking, and a palpable Tendency to humour, approve of, or encreafe the good Opinion Man has of himfelf : As you'll find, on the Contrary, that in the Words Difhonour, Shame, Ignominy, and whatever is difhonourable, there is an Intention, or Something imply'd, to difpleafe and mortify thofe it concerns, on Account of that fame Paffion of Self-liking, and an Endeavour to leffen, contradict or deftroy Self-Efteem, which is that good Opinion which Man has of himfelf from Nature.

Hor. That the Words Honour and Shame are either literally made Ufe of, as you fay, or metaphorically applied to other Creatures or Things inanimate, I believe : I allow likewife, that the Principle of Honour is found in no Breaft that is not poffefs'd of Self-liking to an eminent Degree ; but I don't think that a Fault.

Cleo. The only Fault I have found with the Principle of Honour, is, it's clafhing with the Chriftian Religion. I have told you the
Rea-

Reasons, why the Church of *Rome* thought it her Interest to reconcile them, and make People believe, that they did not interfere with one another. She has always consulted Human Nature, and ever join'd gay Shew and Pomp, as I have hinted before, to Superstition; well knowing, that, as to keep Man under and in Subjection, you must work upon his Fear, so, to make him act with Alacrity, and obey with Pleasure, where Lucre is out of Question, you must flatter his Pride. It is from this Policy of hers, that all Names of Dignity and Distinction among Christians, as Earl, Baron, Duke, Marquis, &c. had originally their Rise as Hereditary Titles. To the same have been owing all the various Ceremonies of Institutions and Instalments; and Coronations, as well as Inthronizations. Of the Orders of Knighthood, and the vast Multiplicity of them, I have spoke already.

Hor. You give more to the Church of *Rome* than her Due: Most Countries in *Christendom* have Orders of Knighthood peculiar to themselves, and of which it is evident, that they were instituted by their own Sovereigns.

Cleo. But look into the Ceremonial of those Institutions, and the great Share the Clergy
has

has in moſt of them, and you'll eaſily ſee, what Stock they ſprung from. And tho' the Sovereign, in every Country, is deem'd to be the Fountain of Honour, yet the Sovereigns themſelves had their Titles, as well as Coats of Arms, from the Popes ; nor had they ever any Enſign of Honour, Power or Authority, which they could depend upon, unleſs it had firſt been granted, or confirm'd and ratify'd, by the See of *Rome.*

Hor. I take the *Inſignia,* which the Proconſuls and Proprietors had in the different Provinces of the *Roman* Empire, and which *Pancirolus* has wrote of ſo amply, to have been much after the Nature of Coats of Arms.

Cleo. Thoſe *Inſignia* belong'd to the Office; and a Governour could only make Uſe of them, whilſt he was in it : But hereditary Coats of Arms, that were given to particular Men or Societies, by Way of Reward for Services perform'd, were never known ; and Heraldry it Self had no Exiſtence, before the Pope's Supremacy had been acknowledged by the Chriſtian World. And if we conſider the fine Opportunities, which the moſt idle and indolent, the moſt inſignificant and unworthy of the Society, often meet with from this Invention of

va-

valuing themfelves upon Actions that were perform'd feveral Ages before they were born, and befpeak a Merit which they know in their Confciences that they are deftitute of; if, I fay, we confider what I have now mention'd, we fhall be forc'd to confefs, that, of all Arts and Sciences, Heraldry has been the moft effectual to ftir up and excite in Men the Paffion of Self-liking, on the fmalleft Foundation; and daily Experience teaches us, that Perfons of Education and Politenefs can tafte no Pleafure in any Thing at Home or Abroad, at Church or the Play-Houfe, where the Gratification of this Paffion is entirely excluded. Of all the Shews and Solemnities that are exhibited at *Rome*, the greateft and moft expenfive, next to a Jubilee, is the Canonization of a Saint. For one that has never feen it, the Pomp is incredible. The Statelinefs of the Proceffions, the Richnefs of Veftments and facred Utenfils that are difplay'd, the fine Painting and Sculpture that are expos'd at that Time, the Variety of good Voices and Mufical Inftruments that are heard, the Profufion of Wax-Candles, the Magnificence which the Whole is perform'd with, and the vaft Concourfe of People, that is occafion'd by thofe

So-

Solemnities, are all such, that it is impossible to describe them.

Hor. It is astonishing, I own; but what would you infer from them ?

Cleo. I would desire you to observe, how vastly different some of the Ends and Purposes are, that Canonizations may be made to serve at the same Time. It is pretended, in the First Place, that they are perform'd to do Justice and pay Veneration to the Memory of those Holy Persons: Secondly, that by Men's worshiping them, they may be induced, among the Rest of the Saints, to intercede with God for the the Sins of their Votaries : And lastly, because it is to be hoped, that among such Numbers as assist at those Solemnities, there are many who will be affected by them, and endeavour to imitate, in their Lives, the holy Examples that are set before them: For there is no Time more seasonable to stir Men up to Devotion and Sentiments of Piety, than when Rapture and high Admiration have been rais'd in them first.

Hor. Besides Canonizations keep up the Reputation of the *Roman* Catholick Faith ; for the new Saints, that are made from Time to Time, are always fresh Witnesses, that Miracles

racles are not ceas'd, and confequently that the Church of *Rome* continues to be the fame Church which *Chrift* and his Apoftles firft eftablifh'd.

Cleo. You are in the Right ; and whilft we confider and give Credit to thofe Pretences, the Defign muft feem to be religious ; and every *Roman* Catholick, who is firm in his Belief, is obliged to think, that whatever Coft is beftow'd upon Canonizations, no Money could be laid out better. But if we mind, on the other Side, the ftrong Sollicitations of the great Men, that either are, or pretend to be the Relations of the venerable Perfon, whofe Holinefs they vouch for ; the vaft Pains that are taken, the Intrigues that are carried on for Years together, to procure this high Favour of the Sacred College ; and when it is obtain'd, what an Honour it is to the whole Family ; the Vifits that are paid from all Parts to every Rich Man that belongs to it, and the Compliments that are made on Account of it; befides the Privileges they receive from it ever after ; If, I fay, we mind thefe Things on the other Side, we fhall find, that in the Motives from which Men fue for this Honour, there is not a Grain of Religion to an Ounce of

Pride,

Pride, and that what feems to be a Solemnity to celebrate the Sanctity of the Dead, is in Reality a Stratagem of the Church to gratify the Ambition of the Living. The Church of *Rome* has never made a Step without Regard to her Temporal Intereſt, and an After-Thought on her Succeſſors. *Luther* and *Calvin*, and ſome Others of the chief Adverſaries of *Rome*, were Men of great Parts, that have gain'd themſelves Immortal Names; but it muſt be confeſs'd, that they rais'd themſelves altogether at the Expence of their Brethren. They gave up both the Patrimony and Dominion of the Church, and made Preſents of them to the Secular Powers, that would eſpouſe their reſpective Cauſes, and eſtabliſh their Doctrines; by which, and the deſtroying of Purgatory, they not only ſtript the Clergy of their Wealth and Power for the preſent, but likewiſe took away the Means by which, one Day or other, it might have been poſſible for their Succeſſors to retrieve them. It is well for the Proteſtant Cauſe, that the Multitude can't hear or know the Wiſhes, that are made in Secret by many of the Clergy, nor the hearty Ejaculations, which the Men of Spirit among them are often ſending after the Memory of
the

the firſt Reformers, for having left their Order in that Pickle, and almoſt at the Mercy of the Laity, after they had been made dependent on the Clergy. If thoſe pious Leaders had underſtood, or at leaſt conſulted Human Nature, they would have known, that ſtrict Lives and Auſterity of Manners don't go by Inheritance, and muſt have foreſeen, that as ſoon as the Zeal of the Reformation ſhould begin to cool both the Clergy and the Laity would relax in their Morals ; and conſequently, that their Succeſſors, after Two or Three Generations, would make wretched Figures, if they were ſtill to continue to preach Chriſtianity without Deceit or Evaſions, and pretend to live conformably to the Rules of it : If they had but reflected on what had happen'd in the Infancy of their Religion, they muſt have eaſily foreſeen what I ſay.

Hor. What is it that happen'd then ?

Cleo. That Chriſt and his Apoſtles taught by Example as well as Precepts the Practice of Humility and the Contempt of Riches ; to renounce the Pomp and Vanity of the World, and mortify the Fleſh, is certain : And that this was ſtriking at the very Fundamentals of Human Nature, is as certain. This could
only

only be perform'd by Men preternaturally affifted; and therefore the Founders of Chriftianity being gone, it could not be expected,
that the fame Aufterity of Life and Self-denial fhould be continued among the Succeffors
of them, as foon as the Miniftry of the Gofpel became a Calling, that Men were brought
up to for a Livelihood; and confidering how
effential thofe mortifying Principles are to
Chriftianity, it is not eafy to conceive, how
the one could be made ftill to fubfift, when
the other fhould ceafe to be. But Nothing
feems more impracticable than that the Gofpel,
in which thofe Principles are evidently taught,
fhould ever be turn'd into an inexhauftible
Fund of Worldly Comforts, Gain, Honour,
and Authority; yet this has been perform'd
by the Skill and Induftry of the Architects,
who have built that Mafter-Piece of Human
Policy, the Church of *Rome.* They have treated Religion as if it was a Manufacture, and
the Church a Set of Workmen, Labourers
and Artificers, of different Employments, that
all contribute and cooperate to produce one
entire Fabrick. In the great Variety of their
Religious Houfes, you have all the Severity
of Manners and Rigour of Difcipline, which
the

the Gofpel requires, improved upon. There
you have perpetual Chaftity, and Virgins
wedded to Chrift : There is Abftinence and
Fafting ; there is Mortifying of the Flefh,
Watching, Praying, the Contempt of Money
and Worldly Honour ; a literal Retirement
from the World, and every Thing you can afk
for, relating to Self-denial, as to Carnal Enjoyments and the renouncing of Pomp and Vanity, at leaft to all outward Appearance. When
Men fee that Strictnefs of Morals, and that
Chriftian Self-denial, which are fo manifeftly
taught in the Gofpel, own'd by the Clergy,
and fome where or other actually comply'd
with, they will eafily give Ear to any Thing
that is faid to them befides. This grand Point
concerning the Aufterity of Life, and mortifying the Flefh, being literally underftood, and
acknowledged by the Clergy to be fuch, as
the Apoftles have deliver'd them without Pre-
varication, it will not be difficult to make the
Laity believe, not only myfterious Contradic-
tions, but likewife the moft palpable Abfurdities ; fuch as Tranfubftantiation ; that the
Pope is infallible, and has the Power of Thun-
dering out *Anathema's* and granting Abfolu-
tions ; and confequently of damning and fav-
ing

ing whom he pleafes; that the Pomp and Magnificence of the Sacred College, and even the Luxury of a Court, are laudable Means, and abfolutely neceffary to keep up the Dignity and outward Luftre of the vifible Church; and that the Spiritual Welfare of it depends upon TemporalAuthority, and cannot be duely taken Care of without large Revenues, Princely Power, Politicks, and Military Force. No Set of Men have deferv'd better of the Church of *Rome*, than the Writers of Legends and the Forgers of Miracles. In the Lives of the Saints, there is a plaufible Reprefentation of the Church Militant; and confidering how naural it is for Man to be fuperftitious, and to love the *Merveilleux*, Nothing could be thought of more agreeable or edifying than to read of fuch Numbers of Holy Men and Women, that did not flinch from Combating themfelves, and to fee the noble Victories that have been obtain'd over the World, the Flefh and the Devil, in a literal Senfe, as are to be met with in thofe judicious Relations.

Hor. But what Analogy is there between the *Roman Catholick* Religion, and a Manufacture, as you infinuated?

Cleo.

Cleo. The Divifion of the whole into fo many different Branches. The great Prelates, of whom not many have any Religion at all, are yet for Worldly Ends continually watching over the Temporal Intereft of it. The little Bifhops and ordinary Priefts take Care of the Myftical Part of it ; whilft the Religious Orders contribute meritorious Works, and feem actually to comply with the harfheft Precepts of Chriftianity, often in a mcre rigid Conftruction than the Words themfelves will bear.

Hor. Then have the Laity no Share in it ?

Cleo. Yes; but their Tafk is the eafieft, and what they club towards Religion chiefly confifts in Faith and Money. But when Men pretend to be Chriftians, and Nothing is to be met with in any Part of their Religion, but what is eafy and pleafant, and Nothing is required either of the Laity or the Clergy, that is difficult to perform, or difagreeable to Human Nature, there is Room to fufpect, that fuch a Set of People lay claim to a Title, that does not belong to them. When Minifters of the Gofpel take Pains to undermine it themfelves, and flatly deny the Strictnefs of Behaviour, and Severity of Manners, that are fo manifeftly inculcated in everyPart of it,I don't won-

wonder, that Men of Sincerity, who can read, fhould refufe to give Credit to every Thing that is faid by fuch Minifters. It is eafier to fpeak with Contempt of the reclufe Lives of the *Carthufians*, and to laugh at the Aufterities of *La Trappe*, than it is to refute what might be alledg'd from the Gofpel to prove the Neceffity there is, that to be acceptable to God, Men fhould fly from Luft, make War with themfelves, and mortify the Flefh. When Minifters of *Chrift* affure their Hearers, that to indulge themfelves in all earthly Pleafures and Senfualities, that are not clafhing with the Laws of the Country, or the Fafhion of the Age they live in, will be no Bar to their future Happinefs, if they enjoy them with Moderation; that Nothing ought to be deem'd Luxury, that is fuitable to a Perfon's Rank and Quality, and which he can purchafe without hurting his Eftate, or injuring his Neighbour; that no Buildings or Gardens can be fo profufely fumptuous, no Furniture fo curious or magnificent, no Inventions for Eafe fo extravagant, no Cookery fo operofe, no Diet fo delicious, no Entertainments or Way of Living fo expenfive as to be Sinful in the Sight of God, if a Man can afford them;

and

and they are the same, as others of the same
Birth or Quality either do or would make
Use of, if they could : That a Man may study and be follicitous about Modes and Fa-
shions, affist at Courts, hunt after Worldly
Honour, and partake of all the Diversions of
the *beau monde*, and at the same Time be a
very good Christian; when Ministers of *Christ*,
I say, assure their Hearers of this, they certainly teach what they have no Warrant for
from his Doctrine. For it is in Effect the
same as to affert, that the strictest Attachment
to the World is not inconsistent with a Man's
Promise of renouncing the Pomp and Vanity
of it.

Hor. But what signify the Austerity of Life
and Forbearance of Nuns and Friars, if they
were real, to all the Rest who don't practise
them ? And what Service can their Self-denial
and Mortification be of to the Vain and Sen-
sual, who gratify every Appetite that comes
uppermost ?

Cleo. The Laity of the *Roman* Communion
are taught and assured, that they may be of
great Service even to the Wicked ; nay, it
may be proved from Scripture, that the In-
tercession of the Righteous and Innocent, is
some-

fometimes capable of averting God's Vengeance from the Guilty. This only wants to be believed ; and it is the eafieft Thing in the World to make the Multitude believe any Affertion, in which there is Nothing that contradicts receiv'd Opinions, and the common Notions which Men have of Things. There is no Truth, that has hitherto been more unanimoufly believed among all Sects and Opinions of Chriftians in all Ages, than that the Gofpel warns Men againft Carnal Pleafures, and requires of them Humility, the Contempt of Earthly Glory, and fuch a Stricthefs of Manners and Morality, as is difficult for Human Nature to comply with. Now when a Clergyman, who pretends to preach the Gofpel, puts fuch Conftructions on the plaineft Texts, in which the Doctrine I fpoke of is literally taught, as can only tend to extenuate and diminifh the Force of them, and when moreover he leaves no Shifts or Evafions untried, till he has deftroy'd the Obfervance of thofe Precepts ; when a Clergyman, I fay, is thus employ'd, it is no Wonder that his Doctrine fhould raife Doubts and Scruples in his Hearers, when they compare it with the common Notions Men have of Chriftianity.

Hor.

Hor. I am no Admirer, you know, of Priefts of any Sort ; but of the Two, I would prefer a Man of Learning and good Senfe, who treats me with good Manners, recommends Virtue, and a reafonable Way of Living, to an ill bred four Pedant, that entertains me with fanatical Cant, and would make me believe, that it is a Sin to wear good Cloaths, and fill my Belly with what I like.

Cleo. There is no Doubt, but the *beau monde*, and all well bred People, that defire to be judged of from outward Appearance, will always chufe the moft eafy *Cafuifts*; and the more ample the Allowances are, which Clergymen give them, of enjoying the World, the more they'll be pleas'd with them. But this can only be of Service amoug the Fafhionable and the Polite, whofe Religion is commonly very fuperficial, and whofe Virtue is feldom extended beyond good Manners. But what will it do to Men of greater Sincerity, that can and dare examine themfelves? What will it do to ferious and able Enquirers, that refufe to truft to Outfides, and will not be barr'd from fearching into the Bottom of Things ? If this was only a Matter of Speculation, a difputable Point in a Ceremony, as
whe-

whether Men are to fit or to ftand at the Performance of it, the Thing might eafily be given up : but it plainly appears to be a Theory fkilfully raifed by Clergymen, to build a Practice upon in their Favour. Thofe eafie Divines don't make fuch large Allowances to others for Nothing: They fpeak one Word for the Laity, and two for themfelves, and feem to have Nothing more at Heart than to enjoy the Benefit of their own Doctrine. It is no Wonder therefore, that fo many of the Clergy are always defirous to converfe with the *beau monde.* Among the beft bred People there is feldom any Difference to be feen between Believers and Unbelievers ; neither of them give any Trouble to their Paftors, and they are all equally cautious of offending. Polite People contradict No body, but conform to all Ceremonies that are fafhionable with Regard to the Time and the Places they are in ; and a courtly Infidel will obferve Decency at Church, and a becoming Carriage there, for the fame Reafon that he does it at a Ball, or in the Drawing-Room.

Hor. As to Indulgences and large Allowances, the *Roman Catholicks* out-do us far, efpecially the *Jefuits*, who certainly are the moft eafy *Cafuifts* in the World.   *Cleo.*

Cleo. They are fo; but it is only in the Management of thofe, whofe Confciences are under their Direction. A Jefuit may tell a Man
fuch or fuch Things are allow'd to Him in
particular, and give him Reafons for it from
his Quality, or the Poft he is in, from the
State of his Health, his Temperament, his
Age, or his Circumftances : But he'll not deny or explain away the Self-denial and the
Mortification in general, that are commanded
in the Gofpel. When you come to this
Point, he'll not leffen the Difficulty and Irk-
fomnefs of Chriftian Duties to Human Nature and the Flefh; but he'll refer you to
the Founder of his Order, and the great Self-
denial he practis'd : Perhaps he'll relate to
you, how that Saint watch'd his Arms all
Night, after he had dedicated them, together
with his Life, to the *Virgin Mary*. But that
the Gofpel requires a literal Mortification of
the Flefh, and other hard Tafks from us, is
the very Bafis which the Pope's Exchequer is
built upon. He could have no Colour for en-
joining Fafting and Abftinence, if it was not
fuppofed, that he had a Warrant for it from
the New Teftament. It is this Suppofition,
that brings all the Grift to his Mill ; and thus

a

a Man may eat Flesh in Lent, without a Sin ;
but tho' he can get the Meat perhaps for Nothing, he shall pay for the Liberty of Eating it.
Buying Absolutions implies the Consciousness
of having committed a Crime ; and No body
would give Money for Indulgencies, if he
thought, that what he desires to be indulged
in, was lawful without them. All Multitudes
will sooner believe a Man to come from God,
who leads an Austere Life himself, and preaches Abstinence and Self-denial to others, tho'
they themselves, I mean the Hearers, don't practise it, or take any Pains to comply with his
Precepts, than they will another, who takes
greater Liberties himself, and whose Doctrine
is less severe. This the wise Architects of the
Church of *Rome*, who were thoroughly skill'd
in Human Nature, were well aware of ; and
accordingly they have improved upon the
Scriptures, and added Lustre to all those Precepts, which it is most difficult to comply
with ; and in commenting on the severest Duties of Christianity, they have been so far
from extenuating and explaining away our
Obligations to perform them, that they have
heighten'd and magnify'd them, not only by
Words and in Theory, but by Practice and
Exam-

Example; as is fo manifeft from the hard and
almoft incredible Tafks, which many of them
have actually impos'd upon themfelves, and
gone through. They have flinch'd at Nothing
on this Head.

Hor. A Man muft be very ftupid to believe,
that his clofe Attachment to the World, and
the Loofnefs of his own Morals can be atton'd
for by the recluse and ftrict Lives that are led
in fome Religious Houfes.

Cleo. Not fo ftupid as you imagine : There
is Nothing in it that clafhes with the common Notions of Mankind. Ceremonies are
perform'd by Proxy ; Men are Security for
one another ; and a Debt is not more effectually difcharg'd, when we receive the Money
from him who borrow'd it, than when it is
paid by his Bail, tho' the Principal himfelf
runs away. If there is but real Self-denial to
be met with any where in a Religion, it is no
difficult Matter to make Multitudes believe,
that they have, or may buy, a Share in it : Befides, all *Roman Catholicks* are brought up in
the firm Belief of the Neceffity there is of Self-
denial. They are ftrictly forbid to eat Flefh
on Fridays; and Pains are taken to infpire
them from their very Childhood with a Hor-
rour

rour againſt the breaking of this Commandment. It is incredible, what Force ſuch a
Precept is of, and how cloſely the Influence
of it ſticks to Men, when it has been earneſt-
ly inculcated to them from their early Youth.
There is no Difficulty in the Thing when they
are grown up ; and I'll engage, that a *Roman*
Catholick, who always has been accuſtom'd
to this Piece of Obſervance till he is Five and
Twenty Years of Age, will find it more eaſy afterwards to continue than to leave it off,
tho' he ſhould turn Proteſtant, or even Turk.

Hor. I have often admired at the great
Force this ſenſeleſs Piece of Superſtition is
of ; for I have ſeen great Reprobates and very looſe Fellows among the *Roman* Catholicks,
who ſtuck at no Manner of Debauchery, and
would often talk prophanely, that yet refuſed
to eat Fleſh on a *Friday*, and could not be
laugh'd out of their Folly ; tho' at the ſame
Time I could ſee, that they were actually a-
ſhamed of it.

Cleo. No Set of People have ſo artfully
play'd upon Mankind as the Church of *Rome*.
In the Uſe they have made of Scripture, they
have conſulted all our Frailties ; and in their
own Interpretations of it, moſt dextrouſly
adap-

adapted themfelves to the common Notions of all Multitudes. They knew perfectly well, not only, that all Men are born with the Fear of an invifible Caufe, but likewife that it is more natural, or, at leaft, that the rude and ignorant of our Species are always more apt to fufpect, that this invifible Caufe is their Enemy, than they are to think it to be their Friend, and will fooner believe it to be an evil and malicious, than a good beneficent Being. To turn this to their Advantage, they made Ufe of all their Skill and Cunning to magnify the Devil, and cry up his Force and Subtlety, his fupernatural Art, his implacable Hatred to Mankind, and great Influence over Human Affairs. All the ftrange Stories they have fpread, the monftrous Fables they have invented, and the grofs Lies they have maintain'd, of Spirits, of Witchcraft, and Apparitions, never had any other Tendency than to manifeft the Works of Satan, and make Every body afraid of his Power and Stratagems at all Times, and in all Places; which has been a prodigious Gain to them. They never taught any Thing that contradicted Vulgar Opinions, and never gave Men any Ideas of Heaven, that were not borrow'd from Something on Earth.

Earth. That Courts of Princes are not deem'd
to be compleat without Women, has advanced
the *Virgin Mary* to be Queen of Heaven.
From the Influence of Mothers, and the Au-
thority they are known to exercise over their
Infants, they have drawn the moſt childiſh
Concluſions to raiſe Superſtition; for to that
Notion, and the great Honour which is every
where allow'd to be due to Parents, it has been
owing, that the Mother of God in the *Roman*
Communion has been all along more addreſs'd
and pray'd to, than her Son; and of the Two
She ſeems to be the more venerable Perſon.
All Patrons in ancient *Rome* had their Clients,
whom they protected; and all Favourites of
Princes have their Creatures, whoſe Intereſt
they eſpouſe upon Occaſion: This has produced the Invocation of Saints and Angels; and
that no Advocates might be wanting in the
Celeſtial Court on any Emergency, the Church
has provided, that there is no Town or Country, no Handicraft or Profeſſion, no Pain or
Diſeaſe, Danger or Diſtreſs, but there is a kind
Saint for that particular Affair, whoſe peculiar Province it is to preſide over and take Care
of every Thing that relates to it; which has
made the Number of them equal with, if not
ſupe-

superiour to that of the Pagan Deities. She knew, that the Incredibility of Things is no Obstacle to Faith among Multitudes; and that in believing of Mysteries, Propositions will not be the less swallow'd for being contradictory to Reason.

Hor. But I thought you was not for keeping Men in Ignorance.

Cleo. What I am for, is not the Question. Priests who would bear an absolute Sway over the Laity, and live luxuriously at their Cost, ought First to make them believe Implicitly: Whereas an honest Clergy, that will teach Nothing concerning Religion, but what is consistent with good Sense, and becoming a rational Creature to believe, ought to deal uprightly with Men throughout the Whole, and not impose upon their Understandings in one Point more than they do in another. From the real Incomprehensibility of God, just Arguments may be drawn for believing of Mysteries that surpass our Capacities. But when a Man has good Reason to suspect, that he who instructed him in these Mysteries, does not believe them himself, it must stagger and obstruct his Faith, tho' he had no Scruples before, and the Things he had been made to believe, are no Ways clashing with his Reason. It is not difficult for a Proteftant Divine to make a Man of Senfe fee the many Abfurdities that are taught by the Church of *Rome*, the little Claim which Popes can lay to Infallibility, and the Prieftcraft there is in what they fay of Purgatory and all that belongs to it. But to perfuade him likewife, that the Gofpel requires no Self-denial, nor any Thing that is irkfome to Nature, and that the Generality of the Clergy of *England* are fincerely endeavouring, in their Lives and Doctrine, to imitate the Apoftles, as nearly as Human Frailty will let them, and is confiftent with the Difference of the Age and Manners between their Time and ours; to perfuade, I fay, a Man of Senfe, that thefe Things are likewife true, would not be fo eafy a Tafk. By a Man of Senfe, I mean a Man likewife of fome Knowledge, who, in the Firft Place, has read the Bible, and believes the Scripture to be the fole Rule of Faith; and, in the Second, is no Stranger to our Church, or any Thing that is openly to be feen relating to her Clergy, efpecially the Heads of them, the Bifhops; fuch as their Palaces and Manner of Living; their Tranflations, Revenues and Earthly Power, together with the Worldly ly Honours, Precedency and other Privileges, which our Spiritual Lords infift upon to be their Due.

Hor. I have often laugh'd my Self at Apoftles in Coaches and Six; but what muft at that Rate the Men of Senfe and Sincerity among the *Roman Catholicks* think of their Prelates, who live in much greater Splendour and Luxury than ours? What muft they think of the Cardinals and the Pope himfelf?

Cleo. Think of them? What they pleafe, fo they dare not to open their Lips againft them, or any Thing which the Clergy are pleas'd to call Sacred. In all *Roman Catholick* Countries, you know, no Books or Pamphlets may be publifh'd, but what are Licenfed; and no Man is allow'd to divulge any Sentiments concerning Religion, that are not entirely Orthodox; which in all Countries, fo regulated, is a vaft Eafe and an unfpeakable Comfort to the Clergy of the eftablifh'd Church.

Hor. I never thought to hear you fpeak againft the Liberty of the Prefs.

Cleo. And you never will; for tho' Orthodoxy and the National Clergy are always the Gainers by thefe Curbs and Prohibitions, yet Truth and Religion are ever the Sufferers by them.

them.   But all prudent Men ought to behave according to the Condition they are in, and the Principles as well as Privileges they lay claim to.   Reform'd Divines own themfelves to be fallible : They appeal to our Reafon, and exhort us to perufe the Scripture Ourfelves. We live in a Country where the Prefs is open; where all Men are at full Liberty to expofe Error and Falfhood, where they can find them ; and No body is debarr'd from Writing almoft any Thing, but Blafphemy and Treafon.   A Proteftant Clergy ought always to remember the Reafons, which their Predeceffors alledg'd for feparating themfelves from the *Roman* Communion, and never to forget, that the Haughtinefs and Luxury of the Prelates, as well as the Covetoufnefs, the Infolence, and barefac'd Encroachments of the Clergy, were a confiderable Part of the Complaints againft Popery. No equitable Guides, that have open'd our Eyes to fee the Frailties of others , ought to expect from us, that in Regard to themfelves we fhould keep them fhut clofe, and never look upon their Behaviour.   The *Roman* Paftors, who keep their Flocks in the Dark, teach them blind Obedience, and never vouchfafe to argue with 'em

any

any more than if they were real Sheep. They
don't advife Men to read the Bible, but fuch
Books of Devotion as their Priefts fhall think
proper for them ; and are fo far from appealing to their Judgment, that they conjure them,
on Pain of Damnation, never to truft their Reafon, but implicitly to believe whatever the
Church fhall require of them.

Hor. You put me in Mind of Father *Canaye,*
the Jefuit in St. *Evremond.* No Reafon ! No
Reafon at all !

Cleo. Where the Clergy are poffefs'd of, and
keep up this Authority over the Laity, and
the Secular Arm is at their Devotion, to punifh whom they condemn, they need not
be nice or circumfpect in their Manner of
Living ; and no Pomp or Luxury will eafily
leffen them in the Efteem of the Multitude.
No Proteftant Clergy have wrote better in Defence of the Reformation than ours ; but
others have certainly gone greater Lengths in
it, as to Worfhip and Difcipline in outward
Appearance. The Difference between the
Roman Catholicks and us feems to be lefs irre-
concilable, than it is between them and the
Reformed Churches of the united *Netherlands*
and *Switzerland*; and I am fully perfuaded,
that

that the Mother Church defpairs not of bringing back to her Bofom this run-away Daugh-
ter of hers, and making this Ifland one Day
or other repay with Intereft the Loffes fhe has
fuftain'd by its long Difobedience. Arguments
alone will never keep out Popery; and *Great
Britain* being once reconciled to the Church
of *Rome*, would add fuch a Weight to her
Power, that it would not be difficult for her
in a little Time to reduce all the Reft of the
Proteftants by main Force, and entirely to Triumph over what She calls the Northern Herefy.

Hor. We have very good Laws to fecure us
from the Ufurpation of *Rome*; and the Ab-
bey Lands, that are in the Poffeffion of the
Laity, I believe, are a better, I mean, a ftronger Argument againft the Return of Popery,
than ever will be fhewn in Print.

Cleo. I believe fo too; but it is not eafy to
determine, what Difficulties and Difcourage-
ments true Politicks and never ceafing Induftry may not furmount in Time. The Church
of *Rome* is never without Men of great Parts
and Application; fhe entertains Numbers of
them; and there is no Government, without
Exception, of which the true Intereft is fo
well underftood, or fo fteadily purfued without Interruption, as hers.   *Hor.*

Hor. But why may not Proteſtants have Men of good Senſe and Capacity among them, as well as *Roman Catholicks?* Do not other Countries produce Men of Genius as well as *Italy* ?

Cleo. Perhaps they do ; tho' none more. The *Italians* are a ſubtle People ; and I believe, that conſummate Knowledge in State Affairs, and Worldly Wiſdom are leſs precarious at *Rome*, than in any other Place you can name. Men of uncommon Genius are not born every Day, no more in *Italy* than any where elſe; but when in other Countries a good Politician goes off the Stage, either of Life or Buſineſs, it is often ſeen that a Bungler ſucceeds him, who in a few Years does more Hurt to the Nation, than the other had Time to do them good in a long Adminiſtration. This never happens at *Rome*; and there is no Court in the Univerſe ſo conſtantly ſupplied with able Managers and crafty Stateſmen as hers : For how ſhort ſoever the Lives of moſt Popes may be, the Sacred College never dies. Tell me now pray, what unlikely Change, what Improbability can you imagine, of which we have not Reaſon to fear, that, if it be poſſible at all, it may be brought about by ſuch a Set of Men ;
when

when every one's private Interest, as well as
that of the Common Cause, are highly concern'd in it, and they are not stinted in Time?

Hor. Assiduity and Patience, I know, will do
strange Things, and overcome great Obsta-
cles. That the Church of *Rome* is more diligent and sollicitous to make Proselytes, than
the Protestants generally are, I have long observed

Cleo. There is no common Cause among
the Reformed : The Princes and Laity of different Persuasions would have been firmly
united long ago, if the Clergy would have suffer'd it; but Divines, who differ, are implacable,
and never known to treat any Adversary with
Temper or Moderation; and it has never
been seen yet, that Two Sects of Christians
did agree, and join heartily in one Interest, unless they were oppress'd, or in immediate Danger of suffering by a common Enemy to both.
As soon as that is over, you always see their
former Animosities revive. If the Church
of *Rome* had no Hopes left, and given over all
Thoughts of ever bringing this Kingdom back
within her Pales, you would see the English
Seminaries abroad neglected and dropt by Degrees; which she now cultivates with the utmost
Care :

Care : For it is from them only, that She can
be furnifh'd with the proper Inftruments to
keep Popery alive in *England*, and buoy up
the drooping Spirits of the diftrefs'd *Catholicks*,
among the many Hardfhips and Difcourage-
ments, they labour under beyond the Reft of
their Fellow-Subjects. Such Offices as thefe, are
every where beft perform'd by Natives: Whatever Perfuafion People are of, if the National
Church of their Country, be not of their
Religion, it is natural to them to wifh it was ;
and that all imaginable Care is taken in the
Englifh Seminaries to encourage, and with
the utmoft Skill to heighten and encreafe this
Natural Defire in thofe under their Care, no
Man can doubt who confiders the Abilities of
the Tutors that are employ'd in them, and the
vaft Advantage the Reduction of *Great Britain* would be to the See of *Rome*. Whilft
thofe Colleges are conftantly fupply'd with
Englifh and *Irifh* Youth, the Popifh Intereft
can never die in this Realm, nor the Church
of *Rome* want infinuating Priefts, or hearty
Zealots, that will act any Part, put on any
Difguife, and run any Rifque for their Caufe,
either in Strengthning the *Roman Catholicks*
that are among us in their Faith, or feducing
Pro-

Proteftants from theirs. No Foreigners could do us half the Mifchief. People love their own Language from the fame Motives as they love their Country ; and there are no Priefts or Clergy, whom Men will fooner hearken to and confide in, than fuch, as take great Pains and exprefs an uncommon Zeal in their Function, at the fame Time that they exercife it at the Hazard of their Liberty or their Lives.The Church of *Rome* has fit Tools for every Work and every Purpofe ; and no other Power upon Earth has fuch a Number of Creatures to ferve it, nor fuch a Fund to reward them when they do. That the Proteftant Intereft loft Ground foon after it was well eftablifh'd, and is ftill declining more and more every Day, is undeniable. To one *Roman Catholick*, that is converted to the Reform'd Religion, Ten Proteftants turn Papifts, among the higheft Quality as well as the Vulgar. What can be the Reafon of this Change ? What is it that this Evil ought to be imputed to ?

Hor. Either the Church of *Rome* is grown more vigilant and mindful of her Caufe fince the Reformation, than She was in *Luther*'s Days, or the Proteftants are become more negligent and carelefs of theirs.

Cleo.

Cleo. I believe both to be true, but especially the latter; for if the Maxims, that were most instrumental in bringing about the Reformation, had been continued, they certainly would have prevented, at least in a great Measure, not only this Evil, but likewise another, which is worse, I mean the Growth of Irreligion and Impiety: Nay, I don't question but the same Maxims, if they were to be tried again would have that Effect still.

Hor. This is a fine Secret, and what, I dare say, the Clergy would be glad to know. Pray, which are those Maxims.

Cleo. The Sanctity of Manners and exemplary Lives of the Reformers, their Application and unwearied Diligence in their Calling; their Zeal for Religion, and Disregard of Wealth and Worldly Enjoyments, either real or counterfeited, for that God only knows.

Hor. I did not expect this. The Bench of Bishops won't thank you for your Prescription: They would call it an Attempt to cure the Patients by blistering the Physicians.

Cleo. Those who would call it so, must be strange Protestant Divines.

Hor. I am sure, that some, if not most of them, would think the Remedy worse than the Disease. *Cleo.*

Cleo. Yet there is none equal to it, no Remedy so effectual, either to cure us of those Evils, and put an entire Stop to, or to hinder and obstruct the Encrease as well of Atheism and Prophaneness, as of Popery and Superstition. And I defy all the Powers of Priestcraft to name such another, a practicable Remedy, of which there is any Probability, that it would go down or could be made use of in a clear-sighted Age, and among a knowing People, that have a Sense of Liberty, and refuse to be Priest-rid. It is amazing, that so many fine Writers among the Clergy, so many Men of Parts and Erudition should seem very earnestly to enquire into the Causes of Libertinism and Infidelity, and never think on their own Conduct.

Hor. But they'll tell you, that you make the Doctrine of the Gospel stricter than it really is; and I think so too; and that you take several Things literally, that ought to be figuratively understood.

Cleo. When Words are plain and intelligible, and what is meant by them in a literal Sense is agreeable to the Tenour and the whole Scope of the Book in which we meet with those Words, it is reasonable to think, that

they

they ought to be literally underſtood. But if, notwithſtanding this, there are others, who are of Opinion, that theſe Words are to be taken in a figurative Senſe, and this figurative Senſe is more forced than the literal, and like-wiſe claſhing with the Doctrine and the Deſign of the Book, we have great Reaſon not to ſide with their Opinion: But if it appears more-over, that thoſe who contend for the forced, figurative Senſe, ſhould be Gainers by it, if their Opinion prevail'd, and it would bring them Profit, Honour, Pleaſure, or Eaſe, then we ought to ſuſpect them to be partial, and the figurative Senſe is to be rejected.

Hor. I don't know what to make of you to Day. You have ſhewn the *Roman Catholick* Religion to be a bare-faced Impoſture; and at the ſame Time you ſeem to blame the *Pro-teſtants* for having left it.

Cleo. I am very conſiſtent with my Self. I have laid open to you the Politicks, Penetra-tion and Worldly Wiſdom of the Church of *Rome,* and the Want of them in the Refor-mers, who expoſed the Frauds of their Ad-verſaries, without conſidering the Hardſhips and Difficulties, which ſuch a Diſcovery would entail upon their Succeſſors. When they par-
ted

ted with their Power, and gave up their Infallibility, they should have foreseen the necessary Consequences of that Honesty and Candour. A Reform'd Church, that will own she may err, must prepare for Heresies and Schisms, look upon them as unavoidable, and never be angry with those who dissent from her. They ought likewise to have known, that no Divines, who will preach the Gospel in its Purity, and teach Nothing but Apostolick Truths without Craft or Deceit, will ever be believ'd long, if they appeal to Men's Reason, unless they will likewise lead, or at least endeavour or seem to lead Apostolick Lives. In all Sects and Schisms it has always been and will ever be observed, that the Founders of them either are, or pretend to be Men of Piety and good Lives; but as there never was a Principle of Morality that Men have set out from, so strict yet, that in Tract of Time Human Nature has not got the better of it, so the Successors of those Founders always become more remiss by Degrees, and look out for Ways and Means to render the Practice of their Doctrine, or the Exercise of their Function, more comfortable and commodious : And all Persuasions have ever lost Ground, and been sunk in their

Re-

Reputation in proportion, as the Teachers of them have relax'd their Manners. No Doctrine ever prevail'd or got any Advantage over the eftablifh'd Religion in any Country, that was not accompanied with a real Aufterity of Life, or a Pretence at leaft to a ftricter Morality, and greater Forbearance, than was generally to be feen in the National Church, at the Time in which the Doctrine was advanced. Thefe are eternal Truths, that muft flow from the Fabrick, the very Effence of Human Nature. Therefore the Clergy may write and preach as they pleafe: They may have all the Skill and Learning that Mortals can be poffefs'd of, and all the Affiftance into the Bargain, that the fecular Power can give them in a free Nation, they will never be able long to keep up their Credit with a mix'd Multitude, if no Shew is made of Self-denial, and they will totally neglect thofe Means, without which that Credit was never acquired.

THE

THE
Third Dialogue
BETWEEN
Horatio and *Cleomenes*.

Horatio.

HO' it is but Two Days ago, that I troubled you almoſt a whole Afternoon, I am come again to ſpend the Remainder of this, and ſup with you, if you are at Leiſure.

Cleo. This is exceeding kind. I am no Ways engaged; and you give me a vaſt Deal of Pleaſure.

Hor. The more I have thought and reflected on what you ſaid of Honour laſt *Tueſday,* the more I have perceiv'd and felt the Truth of it in Spight of my Teeth. But I ſhall never dare to ſpeak of ſo wretched an Origin.

Cleo.

Cleo. The Beginning of all Things relating to Human Affairs was ever fmall and mean : Man himfelf was made of a Lump of Earth. Why fhould we be afhamed of this? What could be meaner than the Origin of Ancient *Rome*? Yet her own Hiftorians, proud as they were, fcrupled not to mention it, after fhe was arrived at the Height of her Glory, and become a Goddefs, *Dea Roma*, to whom Divine Honours were paid throughout the Empire, and a ftately Temple was erected within her own Walls.

Hor. I have often wonder'd at that *Dea Roma*, and her Statues refembling thofe of *Pallas*. What could they pretend her Divinity to confift in?

Cleo. In her vaft Power, which every Freeman had the Privilege to imagine, he had a Share in.

Hor. What a *Bizar*, what a monftrous Humour muft it have been, that could make a wife People fuppofe that to be a Goddefs, which they knew to be a City !

Cleo. Nothing in the Univerfe, but the Pride of the Citizens. But I don't think, that the Humour, which you feem to be fo much aftonifh'd at, is altogether worn off yet. In

Poe-

Poetry, Painting and Sculpture, you fee Rivers, Towns, and Countries continue to be reprefented under the Images of Men and Women as much as ever. Look upon the Marble Figures about the Pedeſtal of Queen *Anne*'s Statue at St. *Paul*'s.

Hor. But No body is fo filly as to worſhip them.

Cleo. Not in outward Shew, becauſe it is out of Faſhion; but the inward Veneration, which is paid by many to the Things reprefented by thoſe Images, is the very fame as it was formerly, and owing to the fame Cauſe.

Hor. In what Part of the World is it, that you have obſerved this?

Cleo. In *Chriſtendom*; Here. If you was to hear a vain Man, that is a confiderable Inhabitant of any large Capital, when he is fpeaking on the Part and in Behalf of his City, *London* for Example, *Paris* or *Amſterdam*, you would find the Honour, the high Eſteem, and the Deference, which in his Opinion are due to it, far fuperiour to any, that are now paid to Mortal Creatures.

Hor. I believe there is a great Deal in what you fay.

Cleo. It is worth your Obſervation, what I

am

am going to mention. Wherever you fee great Power and Authority lodged in a confiderable Number of Men, mind the profound Refpect and Submiffion, each Member pays to the whole, and you'll find, that there is great Plenty, throughout the World, of what you faid, two Days ago, was inconceivable to you.

Hor. What is that, pray ?

Cleo. Idols, that are their own Worfhipers, and fincerely adore themfelves.

Hor. I don't know but there may be, in your Way of conftruing Things : But I came with a Defign to difcourfe with you on another Subject. When you faid in our laft Converfation, that *a peaceful Difpofition and Humility were not Qualities more promifing in the Day of Battle, than a contrite Heart and a broken Spirit are Preparatives for Fighting,* I could not help agreeing with your Sentiments ; yet it is a common Notion, even among Men of very good Senfe, that the beft Chriftians make the beft Soldiers.

Cleo. I verily believe, that there are no better Soldiers, than there are among the Chriftians; and I believe the fame of Painters; but I am well affured, that the beft in either Calling are often far from being the beft Chriftians.

tians. The Doctrine of *Chrift* does not teach
Men to Fight, any more than it does to Paint.
That *Englifhmen* fight well is not owing to
their Chriftianity. The Fear of Shame is able
to make moft Men brave. Soldiers are made
by Difcipline. To make them proud of their
Profeffion, and infpire them with the Love
of Glory, are the fureft Arts to make them
valiant : Religion has Nothing to do with it.
The *Alcoran* bids its Followers fight and pro-
pagate their Faith by Arms and Violence; nay,
it promifes Paradife to All, who die in Battle
againft Infidels ; yet you fee, how often the
Turks have turn'd Tail to the *Germans,* when
the latter have been inferiour in Number.

Hor. Yet Men never fight with greater Ob-
ftinacy than in Religious Wars. If it had not
been taken for granted, that Men were ani-
mated to Battle by Preaching, *Butler* would
never have call'd the Pulpit, *Drum Ecclefiaftick.*

Cleo. That Clergymen may be made Ufe of
as Incendiaries, and by perverting the Duties
of their Function, fet Men together by the
Ears, is very true ; but no Man was ever made
to fight by having the Gofpel preach'd to him.
From what I have faid of Self-liking and Human Nature, the Reafon is manifeft, why
among

among People, that are indifferent to one another, it is a difficult Task to make a Man sincerely love his Neighbour, at the same Time, that it is the easiest Thing in the World to make him hate his Neighbour with all his Heart. It is impossible that Two distinct Persons or Things should be the same ; therefore they must all differ in Something.

Hor. Cannot Two Things be so exactly alike, that they shall differ in Nothing ?

Cleo. No : For if they are Two, they must differ in Situation, East and West, the Right and the Left; and there is Nothing so small, so innocent, or so insignificant, that Individuals of our Species can differ in, but Self-liking may make a Handle of it for Quarrelling. This close Attachment and Partiality of every Man to himself, the very Word, Difference, points at, and upbraids us with: For tho' literally it is only a Term, to express that Things are not the same ; yet, in its figurative Sense, Difference between Men signifies Disagreement in Opinions, and Want of Concord. For not only different Nations, but different Cities in the same Kingdom, different Wards, different Parishes, different Families, different Persons, tho' they are Twins, or the best Friends

in

in the World, are all in a fair Way of Quarrelling, whenever the Difference, that is between them, be that what it will, comes to be look'd into and difcufs'd; if both act with Sincerity, and each Party will fpeak from the Bottom of their Hearts.

Hor. Self is never forgot; and I believe, that many love their Country very fincerely for the Sake of One.

Cleo. Nay, what is all the World to the meaneft Beggar, if he is not to be confider'd as a Part of it?

Hor. This is a little too openly inculcated at Church; and I have often wonder'd, how a Parfon, preaching before a few Clowns in a pitiful Village, fhould, after he has named all the great People in the Nation, pray God to blefs more *efpecially* the Congregation there affembled; and this at the fame Time that the King and the Royal Family are at Prayers likewife; and the Houfe of Lords at one Church, and the Houfe of Commons at another. I think it is an impudent Thing for a Parcel of Country Boobies to defire to be ferv'd firft, or better, than fo many Hundred Congregations, that are fuperiour to them in Number and Knowledge, as well as Wealth and Quality.

Cleo.

Cleo. Men always join moſt heartily in Petitions, in which they manifeſtly have a Share; and that the *Eſpecially*, you find Fault with, was put in from that Conſideration, I believe No body denies.

Hor. But there ſeems to be a low Artifice, a crafty Deſign, by which the Compilers of thoſe Prayers, knowingly made People lay a Streſs upon a Thing, in which there is no Reality. When I hear a Man pray for Bleſſings on All, eſpecially the Congregation where I am preſent, it pleaſes me well enough, and the Word *Eſpecially*, has its Effect upon me whilſt I think no further; but when I conſider, that the ſame Words are ſaid to every Audience of the ſame Church throughout the Kingdom, I plainly find that I was pleas'd with Nothing.

Cleo. Suppoſe I ſhould own, that it was a Contrivance of thoſe, who compoſed the Prayers, to raiſe Devotion, and that this Contrivance had been the Effect of a thorough Knowledge of Human Nature; where would be the Harm, ſince No body can be injured by it? But to return to our Subject. If Difference in the leaſt Things is capable of raiſing Anger, there is no Doubt, but it will do

it

it moſt in Things that are very material, and
of the higheſt Concern: And that Religion in
all Countries is an Affair of the greateſt Concern, is taken for granted by all good Men, and
ſeldom denied by the bad. This is the Reaſon, that in Religious Wars Men are more in-
veterate, and commit more Cruelties, than
when they fight upon any other Account.
Here the worſt and moſt vicious Men have
fine Opportunities of gratifying their natural
Malice and Rancour of Heart, without being
blamed for it; and placing a Merit in doing
Miſchief. Therefore we ſee, that thoſe, who
are moſt neglectful of their Duty, and act
moſt contrary to the Dictates of their Religion, are ſo often the moſt zealous in fighting
for it. There are other Things that help, and
all contribute, to make Religious Wars the
moſt bloody. Men are commonly ſure of Nothing ſo much, as they are of the Truth of the
Religion they profeſs; ſo that in all Religious
Quarrels, Every body is ſatisfied that he has
Juſtice on his Side: This muſt make Men
obſtinate. The Multitude in all Countries
aſcribe to the Deities they worſhip the
ſame Paſſions which they feel themſelves;
and knowing how well pleas'd they are with
Every

Every body that is on their Side, and will take their Part, they expect their Reward from Heaven, which they feem to defend; and on that Score they think with Delight on the Loffes and Calamities which they make others fuffer; whether *Churchmen* fight with *Prefbyterians, Papifts* with *Proteftants,* or *Mahometans* with *Chriftians* of any Sort. Thofe who are of Opinion, that the beft *Chriftians* make the beft Soldiers, have commonly their Eyes on the Civil Wars both in *France* and in *England.*

Hor. And if you compare the Prince of *Conde's* Army with that of the League there, or *Cromwell's* Troops with the King's Forces here, the *Whigs* will tell you, that in either Nation you may meet with fufficient Proofs, to confirm the Opinion you fpeak of.

Cleo. I have Nothing to do with *Whigs* or *Tories*; but let us narrowly look into this Affair, and examine it impartially. Religion was brought into the Quarrel, you know, in both Kingdoms, and the Cafes between the Adverfaries here and there were much the fame. The *Huguenots* and *Roundheads* on the one Side faid, that they had Nothing fo much at Heart as Religion; that the National Worfhip was

Ido-

Idolatry; that Chriſtianity required no out-
ward Shew of Altars or Veſtments, but the
Sacrifice of the Heart to be ſeen in Men's
Lives; that God was to be ſerv'd with greater
Strictneſs, than was obſerved by the National
Clergy; that they fought his Cauſe, and did
not queſtion, but by his Help to obtain the
Victory. The *Leaguers* and *Cavaliers* ſaid on
the other Side, that Lay-men, eſpecially Soldiers, were improper Judges in Matters of
Religion; that themſelves were honeſt Men,
loyal Subjects, who fought for the eſtabliſh'd
Church, their King and Country; and as to
their Adverſaries, that they were a Parcel of
Hypocritical Raſcals, that under the Maſk of
Sanctity carried on an open Rebellion, and had
no other Deſign than to dethrone the King,
and get the Government into their own Clut-
ches. Let us ſee the Conſequence that would
naturally follow from this Difference. The
Firſt, to ſupport their Cauſe, would think it
neceſſary not to be too glaringly inconſiſtent
with themſelves; therefore they would diſplay
ſomewhat more of Devotion, and by praying
often, and perhaps ſinging of Pſalms, make
a greater Shew of Religion, than is commonly ſeen in Armies. Should the Chief of ſuch
                                            Troops

Troops, and the great Men under him, who are moft likely to get by the Quarrel, be more circumfpect in their Actions, and attend Divine Worfhip oftner than is ufual for Perfons of Quality, their Example would influence the inferiour Officers, and thefe would take Care, that the Soldiers fhould comply, whether they would or not. If this was well perform'd on the one Side, it is very natural to fuppofe, that the other, knowing the firft to be no better Men than themfelves, and believing them to be Hypocrites, would not only be offended at their Behaviour, but likewife, in Oppofition to their Enemies, be more neglectful of Religious Duties, than well difciplin'd Armies generally are, and the Soldiers allow'd to be more diffolute in their Lives than is ufual. By this Means the Contraft between two fuch Armies, would be very confpicuous. A good Politician may add to, or take from the Principle of Honour, what Virtue or Qualification he pleafes ; and a fkilful General, who can guard his own Actions, and will be at fome Trouble in Self-denial where he may be obferved, may model an Army as he thinks fit. All Superiours, in Camps as well as Courts, will ever ferve for

Pat-

Patterns to their Inferiours ; and fhould Officers unanimoufly refolve to render Swearing
unfafhionable, and in good Earneft fet about
this Task, by Example as well as Precept and
Difcipline, it would not be difficult to ma-
nage Soldiers in fuch a Manner, that in lefs
than Half a Year not an Oath fhould be heard
among them. If there were Two Armies in
the fame Country, and of the fame Nation, in
one of which the Soldiers fhould curfe and
fwear, as much as is commonly done among
all loofe and ill-bred People, and in the other
the Men fhould have been cured of that bad
Cuftom, it is incredible what Reputation of
being Good and Religious, thofe, who would
only forbear Swearing, would gain beyond
their Adverfaries, tho' they were equally guilty with them of Whoring, Drinking, Gaming,
and every other Vice except that one. Therefore if one General, to pleafe and keep in with
a Party, fhould think it his Intereft that his
Troops fhould make a greater Appearance of
Godlinefs, than is commonly obferved among
Military Men ; and another, to pleafe a contrary Party, fhould take it to be his Intereft to
act as contrary as it was poffible to what
his Enemies did, and endeavour to be the
Re-

Reverse of them, the Difference would be prodigious.

Hor. Then if in one Army they were Valiant, the General of the other would endeavour to make his Men Cowards.

Cleo. They would differ in every Thing that Soldiers can differ in : The Obfervance of the Point of Honour and Hatred to their Enemies are infeparable from their Calling ; therefore refenting of Affronts among themfelves, and cruel Ufage to their Enemies, were not more banifh'd from the Armies of the *Huguenots* and *Roundheads*, than they were from thofe of the *Leaguers* and *Cavaliers*.

Hor. The true Reafon of the Difference, in the Lives and Morals of the Soldiers, between the King's Forces and the Rebels, was the Difference of their Circumftances, and the Care that was taken of them. The Parliament's Army was regularly provided for, and always able to pay for what they had. But the others, who were moft commonly in Want, were forced to live upon the Country, and take their Provifions where they could get them ; and this will make all Troops more diffolute and diforderly, than is confiftent with the Service, tho' they had the beft Officers in the World.

Cleo.

Cleo. The Misfortune you fpeak of, and which the King's Army labour'd under, muft every where be a great Hinderance to Difcipline; and I verily believe, that his Soldiers fuffer'd very much in their Morals on Account of it; but I am perfuaded, that the Contrariety of Principles, which I hinted at, was an Addition to that Misfortune, and made it worfe; for that the *Cavaliers* laughed at the *Roundheads* for their praying fo long and fo often, and the great Shew they made of Devotion, is certain; and there is always a Pleafure in appearing to be the Reverfe of what we ridicule in our Enemies. But whatever was then, or might at any other Time, be the true Reafon of the Difference in the Shew of Piety and Goodnefs between two fuch Armies, let us fee the Confequence of it, and the Effect it would naturally have on the fober Party. All Multitudes are fuperftitious; and among great Numbers, there are always Men prone to Enthufiafm; and if the Pretenders to Godlinefs had skilful Divines (as no doubt, they would have)that knew,how to extol the Goodnefs and Piety of the General and the Soldiers, declaim againft the Wickednefs and reprobate Lives of the Enemies, and remonftrate

ftrate to their Hearers, how God muft love the firft, and, from his known Attributes, hate the latter, it would in all Probability produce every Thing we read of in the Armies of the Prince of *Conde* and the Parliament. Some Colonels would preach, and fome Soldiers would learn Prayers and Scraps of Pfalms by Heart, and many of them would grow more circumfpect in indulging their Vices, than is common to Men of their Function. This latter would make the Men more governable, and confequently better Troops, and all together would make a great Noife. Befides, Mankind are fo given to flatter themfelves, that they'll believe any Thing, that is faid in their Praife; and fhould, in any Regiment of fuch an Army, the Chaplain difplay his Eloquence before a Battle, exhort the Men to Bravery, fpeak in Commendation of the Zeal and Piety of the Officers and the Troops in general, and find out fome particular Reafon, why God fhould love and have Regard for that Regiment beyond any other, it might have a very good Effect upon the moft Wicked, as well as the better Sort. And if this Chaplain, from what he knew of them, fhould pathetically encourage them, and promife them the Victory,

En-

Enthufiafm is fo catching, that a Fellow, who lay with a Whore over Night, and was drunk the Day before, if he faw his Comrades moved, might be tranfported with Joy and Eagernefs to fight, and be ftupid enough to think, that he had a Share in God's Favour. The *Greek* and *Roman* Hiftories abound with Inftances of the immenfe Ufe that may be made in War of Superftition well turn'd: The groffeft, if fkilfully managed, may make the fearful, undaunted, and the loofeft Livers exert themfelves to the utmoft of their Power, from a firm Belief, that Heaven is on their Side. That Superftition has had this Effect upon Men of almoft every Perfuafion, as well as Heathen Idolaters, is certain; but he muft be a notable Divine, that can expect the fame from the Doctrine of *Chrift*, faithfully deliver'd, and preach'd in its Purity. It is poffible therefore that any Number of Troops may, by crafty Declamations and other Arts, be made Zealots and Enthufiafts, that fhall fight and pray, fing Pfalms one Hour, and demolifh an Hofpital the next; but you'll as foon meet with an Army of Generals or of Emperours, as you will with, I won't fay an Army, but a Regiment, or even a Company of good Chriftians among

Mi-

Military Men. There never were better Troops, or Men that behaved with greater Gallantry and Chearfulnefs, than we had in the two laft Wars; Officers as well as common Soldiers; but I would as foon believe, that it was Witchcraft that made them brave, as that it was their Religion.

Hor. Yet I have often heard it from experienc'd Officers, that the moft virtuous, the fobereft, and the moft civiliz'd Fellows made the beft Soldiers, and were thofe whom they could moft depend upon.

Cleo. I heartily believe that to be true for the Generality; for I know, that by Virtuous, you don't mean much more than tolerably Honeft, fuch as are not given to wrong or deceive Any body; or elfe among the Officers themfelves, you know, that very Few of them are poffefs'd of many Chriftian Virtues, or would be fond of the Character. Do but confider what is required of a Soldier. There are Three Things which the Officers are chiefly afraid of in their Men: The Firft is, that they may defert, which is fo much Money loft: The Second, that they may rob or fteal, and fo come to be hang'd: The Third is, that they may be fick, and confequently in-

incapable of doing Duty. Any middling Honefty fecures them entirely as to the two Firft; and, without Doubt, the lefs vicious, that is, the more fober and temperate the Men are, the more likely they are to preferve their Health. As for the Reft, Military Men are eafy *Cafuifts* for the Generality, and are ufed to give, as well as take, large Grains of Allowance. A Soldier, who minds his Bufinefs, is feldom reproved for taking any Pleafure he can come at, without being complain'd of: And if he be brave, and underftands his Exercife, takes Care always to be fober when he is upon Duty, pays a profound Refpect to his Officers, as well as a ftrict Obedience to their Commands, watches their Eyes, and flies at a Nod, he can never fail of being beloved. And if moreover he keeps himfelf clean, and his Hair powder'd, is neat in his Cloaths, and takes Care not to be pox'd; let him do what he pleafes for the Reft, he'll be counted a very valuable Fellow. A Man may do all this without Chriftianity, as well as he can do it without having an Eftate. There are Thoufands that are lefs circumfpect and not half fo well accomplifh'd, who yet are well efteem'd in that Station. And as I have allow'd on the
one

one Hand, that the foberest and the most civiliz'd Fellows make the best Soldiers, and
are, generally speaking, the most to be depended upon in an Army, so it is undeniable on
the other, that, if not the major, at least a
very considerable Part of our best Troops,
that had the greatest Share in the Victories
we obtain'd, was made up of loose and immoral, if not debauch'd and wicked Fellows.
Nay, I insist upon it, that Jayl-birds, Rogues,
who had been guilty of the worst of Crimes,
and some that had been saved from the Gallows to recruit our Forces, did on many Occasions both in *Spain*, and *Flanders*, fight with
as much Intrepidity, and were as indefatigable,
as the most Virtuous amongst them. Nor
was this any Thing strange or unexpected; or
else the recruiting Officers ought to have been
punish'd, for listing and giving the Money of the
Publick to Men, of whom there was no Probability that they could be made Soldiers. But
to make it evident, how little the Religion
and Morality of a Soldier are minded by his
Superiours, and what great Care is taken to
keep up and cultivate his Pride ———.

Hor. That latter I have seen enough of in
the

150 *The Third Dialogue.*

the *Fable* of the *Bees.* You would speak about the Cloaths and Accoutrements.

Cleo. I wave them ; tho' there it is likewise very conspicuous. I only desire you to compare the Things he is indulg'd in, and which, if he pleases, he may brag of, with what he is taught to be ashamed of, the grand Offence, which, if once committed, is never to be pardon'd. If he has but Courage, and knows how to please his Officers, he may get drunk Two or Three Times a Week, have a fresh Whore every Day, and swear an Oath at every Word he speaks, little or no Notice shall be taken of him to his Dishonour ; and, if he be good humour'd, and forbears stealing among his Comrades, he'll be counted a very honest Fellow. But if, what *Christ* and his Apostles would have justify'd him in and exhorted him to do, he takes a Slap in the Face, or any other gross Affront before Company, without resenting it, tho' from his intimate Friend, it cannot be endured; and tho' he was the soberest, and the most chaste, the most discreet, tractable and best temper'd Man in the World, his Business is done. No body will serve with a noted Coward; nay, it would be an Affront to desire it of Gentlemen Soldiers,

diers, who wear the King's Cloth; and the Officers are forc'd to turn him out of the Regiment. Thofe who are unacquainted with Military Affairs and Chaplains of Regiments, would not imagine, what a fmall Portion of Virtue and Forbearance a Soldier ftands in Need of, to have the Reputation of a good religious Man among thofe he converfes with. Clergymen, that are employ'd in Armies, are feldom rigid *Cafuifts*; and Few of them are Saints themfelves. If a Soldier feems to be lefs fond of ftrong Liquors than others generally are; if he is feldom heard to Swear; if he is cautious in Love-Affairs, and not openly vicious that Way; if he is not known to Steal or Pilfer, he'll be ftiled a very honeft, fober Fellow. But if, moreover, fuch a one fhould behave with Decency at Divine Service, and feem now and then to be attentive to what is fpoken; if ever he had been feen with a Book in his Hand, either open or fhut; if he was refpectful to the Clergy, and zealous againft thofe, who are not of the fame Religion which he profeffes to be of, he would be call'd a very Religious Man; and half a Dozen of them in a Regiment would, in a little Time, procure a mighty Character to the whole, and great Honour to the Chaplain. *Hor.*

Hor. I dare fay, that on fome Occafions he would take the Liberty from it to brag, that there were no better Chriftians in the World, than a great many were, whom he had under his Care.

Cleo. Confidering how Things are often magnify'd without Regard to Truth or Merit, and what Advantages fome Men will take, right or wrong, to advance as well as maintain the Caufe they get by; it is not improbable, that three or four fcore thoufand Men, that were kept in good Difcipline, tho' they were all taken at Random from the loweft and idleft of the Vulgar, might be ftiled an Army of good Chriftians, if they had a Chaplain to every Regiment, and but Two or Three fuch orderly Soldiers, as I have defcrib'd, in every Thoufand : And I am perfuaded, that the Sect or Religion, which they pretended to follow and profefs, would, by the Help of able and active Divines, acquire more Credit and Reputation from thofe Few, than all the Loofnefs, Debauchery and grofs Vices of the Reft would ever be able to take away from them.

Hor. But from what you have faid, I fhould think, that the Gofpel muft do Hurt among fighting Men. As fuch they muft be animated

red by another Spirit, and can receive no Benefit from the Doctrine of Peace. What Occasion is there for Divines in an Army?

Cleo. I have hinted to you several Times, that in the Management of Human Creatures, the Fear of an invisible Cause, which they are all born with, was always to be consulted; and that no Multitudes can ever be govern'd, so as to be made useful to any one Purpose, if those, who attempt to rule over them, should neglect to take Notice of, or but any Ways seem to slight the Principle of that Fear. The worst of Men are often as much influenc'd by it as the best; or else Highwaymen and Housebreakers would not swear Fidelity to one another. God is call'd upon as a Witness to the mutual Promises of the greatest Miscreants, that they will persevere in their Crimes and Villanies, and to the last Drop of their Blood be unalterably Wicked. This, you know, has been done in Massacres, the blackest Treasons, and the most horrid Conspiracies; tho' the Persons concern'd in them, perhaps, gave other Names to their Undertakings. By this we may see, what absurd Notions Men may have of the Deity, who undoubtedly believe his Existence: For how flagitious soever Men are, none can be deem'd
Atheists

Atheifts but thofe, who pretend to have abfolutely conquer'd, or never been influenced by
the Fear of an invifible Caufe, that over-rules
Human Affairs ; and what I fay now has been
and ever will be true in all Countries, and in
all Ages, let the Religion or Worfhip of the
People be what they will.

Hor. It is better to have no Religion, than
to worfhip the Devil.

Cleo. In what Refpect is it better ?

Hor. It is not fo great an Affront to the
Deity not to believe his Exiftence, as it is to
believe him to be the moft Cruel and the moft
Malicious Being that can be imagin'd.

Cleo. That is a fubtle Argument, feldom
made Ufe of but by Unbelievers.

Hor. Don't you think, that many Believers
have been worfe Men, than fome *Atheifts* ?

Cleo. As to Morality, there have been good
and bad Men of all Sects and all Perfuafions ;
but before we know any Thing of Men's Lives,
Nothing can be worfe in the Civil Society,
than an Atheift, *cæteris paribus.* For it would
be ridiculous to fay, that it is lefs fafe to truft
to a Man's Principle, of whom we have fome
Reafon to hope, that he may be with-held by
the Fear of Something, than it is to truft to

one,

one, who abfolutely denies, that he is with-held by the Fear of any Thing. The old *Mexicans* worfhip'd *Vitzliputzli*, at the fame Time that they own'd his Malice, and execra-ted his Cruelty; yet it is highly probable, that fome of them were deterr'd from Perjury for Fear of being punifh'd by *Vitzliputzli*; who would have been guilty of it, if they had not been afraid of any Thing at all.

Hor. Then not to have believed the Exif-tence of that chimerical Monfter was Athe-ifm in *Mexico*.

Cleo. It certainly was among People that knew of no other invifible Caufe.

Hor. But why fhould I wonder at the *Mex-icans*? There are Chriftians enough, of whom, to judge from their Sentiments and Behaviour, it is hard to determine, which it is they are moft afraid of, God or the Devil.

Cleo. I don't queftion, but among the Vul-gar, more Perfons have been deterr'd from do-ing Evil, by what they had heard of the Tor-ments of Hell, than have been made virtuous by what had been told them of the Joys of Heaven, tho' both had been reprefented to them as equally infinite and unutterable.

Hor. But to return to my Queftion. When

I

I afk'd what Occafion there was for Divines in an Army, I was not ignorant of the Neceſſity there is of having Religion and Prieſts of ſome Sort or other, to humour as well as awe the Multitude ; but I wanted to know the Myſte-ry, and be let into the Secret, by which the Doctrine of Peace is made ſerviceable to the carrying on of War ; for that Preachers of the Goſpel have not only exhorted Men to Bat-tle, but likewiſe that they have done it effec-tually ; and that Soldiers have been inſpired with Courage, and made to fight with Obſti-nacy by their Sermons, the Hiſtory of almoſt every Country can witneſs.

Cleo. A little Accuracy will ſet us to Rights. That what you ſay has been, and is often done by Sermons and Preachers, both Proteſtant and Popiſh, is certainly true. But I deny, that ever it was once done by a Preacher of the Goſpel.

Hor. I don't underſtand your Diſtinction. Are not all Chriſtian Divines call'd Preachers, as well as Miniſters of the Goſpel ?

Cleo. But many People are call'd, what, ſtrictly ſpeaking, they are not. The Reaſon I have for what I ſay is, that there is Nothing contain'd in the Goſpel, that can have the leaſt

Ten-

Tendency to promote or juſtify War or Diſ-cord, Foreign or Domeſtick, Publick or Pri-vate; nor is there any the leaſt Expreſſion to be found in it, from which it is poſſible to ex-cite or ſet People on to quarrel with, do Hurt to, or any Ways offend one another, on any Account whatever.

Hor. But this encreaſes the Myſtery, and makes the Fact leſs intelligible.

Cleo. I will unfold it to you. As all Prieſts have ever maintain'd, that they were the In-terpreters of the Will of the Deity they pre-tended to ſerve, and had an undoubted Right of conſtruing and explaining the Doctrine and the Meaning of the Religion they taught and preſided over: As, I ſay, all Prieſts have ever maintain'd this, ſo the Chriſtian Clergy, as ſoon as they took it in their Heads to be Prieſts likewiſe, claim'd the ſame Privilege; and finding ſeveral Things, which they had a Mind to, denied them in the Goſpel; and that many Conveniencies, which all other Prieſts had ever, not only been fond of, but likewiſe enjoy'd, were in expreſs Words forbid, and abſolutely prohibited in the *New Teſtament*, they had Recourſe to the *Old*, and provident-ly took Care from thence to ſupply the Defi-ciency of the *New*.   *Hor.*

Hor. So, when they had no fetrled Revenue or Pomp of Drefs from the Gofpel, they took up with the Tithes and Sacerdotal Ornaments of the *Levites,* and borrow'd from the *Jewish* Priefts and Prophets every Thing that was worth having.

Cleo. This would open too large a Field, and therefore I would look into the Clergy's Behaviour no farther, than as it relates to Armies and military Men, and take Notice, that whenever Pillage or fhedding of Blood are to be juftified or encouraged by a Sermon, or Men are to be exhorted to Battle, to the Sacking of a City or the Devaftation of a Country, by a pathetick Difcourfe, the Text is always taken from the *Old Teftament* ; which is an inexhauftible Fund for Declamation on almoft every Subject and every Occafion : And there is no worldly End, which the moft ambitious Man, or the moft cruel Tyrant can have to ferve, but from fome Part or other of that Book a Divine of middling Capacity may find out a proper Text to harangue upon, that fhall anfwer the Purpofe. But to make it evident, that Divines may be ufeful to all Fighting Men, without preaching of the Gofpel, we need but to confider, that among all the Wars

and

and Diffentions, which Chriftians have had
with one another on innumerable Accounts,
there never was a Caufe yet, fo unreafonable
or abfurd, fo unjuft or openly wicked, if it
had an Army to back it, that has not found
Chriftian Divines, or at leaft fuch as ftiled
themfelves fo, who have efpoufed and call'd
it Righteous. No Rebellion was ever fo unnatural, nor Tyranny fo cruel, but if there
were Men who would fight for it, there were
Priefts who would pray for it, and loudly
maintain, that it was the Caufe of God. Nothing is more neceffary to an Army, than to
have this latter ftrenuoufly infifted upon, and
fkilfully inculcated to the Soldiers. No body
fights heartily, who believes himfelf to be in
the wrong, and that God is againft him:
Whereas a firm Perfuafion of the Contrary,
infpires Men with Courage and Intrepidity; it
furnifhes them with Arguments to juftify the
Malice of their Hearts, and the implacable
Hatred they bear their Enemies; it confirms
them in the ill Opinion they have of them, and
makes them confident of Victory; *fi Deus pro
nobis quis contra nos?* In all Wars it is an everlafting Maxim in Politicks, that whenever Religion can be brought into the Quarrel, it
ought

ought never to be neglected, and that how
fmall foever the Difference may be between
the contending Parties, the Divines on each
Side, ought to magnify and make the moft of
it; for Nothing is more comfortable to Men,
than the Thought, that their Enemies are
likewife the Enemies of God.

Hor. But to make Soldiers laborious as well
as governable, would it not be ufeful to exhort them to Virtue, and a clofe Attachment
to the Principle of Honour?

Cleo. The Principle of Honour is never forgot; and as to Virtue, what is required of them
is Fortitude, and to do as they are bid. And
if you'll 'confider what Pains are taken to
make them afhamed of Cowardice above
all other Vices; and how prompt, as well as
fevere, the Punifhment for Difobedience is in
the leaft Trifles among Soldiers, beyond what
it is any where elfe; if, I fay, you'll confider
thefe Things on the one Hand, and on the
other the great Latitude that is given them
as to Morals, in what has no Regard to the
Service, you'll find, that for the Firft, Divines
are not wanted, and that for the other they
can do but little Good. However Morality is
often preach'd to them, and even the Gofpel

at

at feafonable Times, when they are in Winter Quarters, or in an idle Summer, when there is no Enemy near, and the Troops perhaps are encamped in a Country, where no Hoftilities fhould be committed. But when they are to enter upon Action, to befiege a large Town, or ravage a rich Country, it would be very impertinent to talk to them of Chriftian Virtues; doing as they would be done by; loving their Enemies, and extending their Charity to all Mankind. When the Foe is at Hand, the Men have Skirmifhes with him every Day, and perhaps a main Battle is expected; then the Mafk is flung off; not a Word of the Gofpel, nor of Meeknefs or Humility; and all Thoughts of Chriftianity are laid afide entirely. The Men are prais'd and buoy'd up in the high Value they have for themfelves: Their Officers call them Gentlemen and Fellow-Soldiers; Generals pull off their Hats to them; and no Artifice is neglected that can flatter their Pride, or infpire them with the Love of Glory. The Clergy themfelves take Care at fuch Times, not to mention to them their Sins, or any Thing that is melancholy or difheartning: On the Contrary, they fpeak chearfully to them, encourage

and

and affure them of God's Favour. They take Pains to juftify, and endeavour to encreafe the Animofities and Averfion, which thofe under their Care have againft their Enemies, whom to blacken and render odious, they leave no Art untried, no Stone unturn'd ; and no Calumny can be more malicious, no Story more incredible, nor Falfity more notorious, than have been made Ufe of knowingly for that Purpofe by Chriftian Divines, both *Proteftants*, and *Papifts*.

Hor. I don't ufe to be an Advocate for Bigots of any Sort, much lefs for Fanaticks, whom I hate ; but Facts are ftubborn Things. It is impoffible to reflect on the fharp and bloody Engagements in the Rebellion, and the Devotion of *Cromwell*'s Army, without being convinced, that there muft have been Men at that Time, that were both Valiant and Religious. It is certain, that the Rebels fought well, and that they had more Days of Fafting and Humiliation, than ever were known among any other Soldiers.

Cleo. That there was a greater Appearance of Religion among them, than ever was among any other regular Troops, I allow; but that none of it could proceed from a Principle of Chriftianity is demonftrable. *Hor.*

Hor. They had Men of unqueſtionable Honour among them; and ſome of them muſt have been ſincere.

Cleo. A great many, I verily believe, were ſincere; but let us look into this Affair a little more narrowly. What do you think of the General? Do you think, that *Cromwell* was a good Chriſtian and a pious Man, who had Nothing ſo much at Heart as Religion and Liberty, and, void of Selfiſhneſs, had devoted himſelf to procure Happineſs Eternal as well as Temporal to the People of *England*? Or that he was a vile wicked Hypocrite, who, under the Cloak of Sanctity, broke through all Human and Divine Laws to aggrandize himſelf, and ſacrifis'd every Thing to his own Ambition, and the Intereſt of his Family?

Hor. There is no Doubt, but all impartial Men muſt believe the latter. But then he underſtood Mankind very well; his very Enemies, that were his Contemporaries, allow'd him to be a Man of great Parts. If he had had the the ſame Opinion of Chriſtianity, which you have, and the Unfitneſs of it to make Men quarrel and fight with Obſtinacy, he would never have made Uſe of it among his Soldiers.

Cleo.

Cleo. And it is as clear as the Sun, that he never did.

Hor. That his Pretences to Religion were no more than Hypocrify, I have allow'd ; but it does not appear, that he defired others to be Hypocrites too : On the Contrary, he took Pains, or at leaft made Ufe of all poffible Means to promote Chriftianity among his Men, and make them fincerely Religious.

Cleo. You will never diftinguifh between Chriftianity, that is, the Doctrine of Chrift, and the Interpretations, that are made of it by Clergymen ; tho' I have often fhew'd you the great Difference there is between them. *Cromwell* was a Man of admirable good Senfe, and thoroughly well acquainted with Human Nature ; he knew the mighty Force of Enthufiafm, and made Ufe of it accordingly. As to Strictnefs of Religion and the Love of Liberty, they had all along been the darling Pretences of the Party he engaged in. The Complaints of the *Puritans* againft Epifcopacy, and that the Church of *England* was not fufficiently reformed, began in Queen *Elizabeth*'s Time, and were very near as old as the Reformation it felf. The People's Murmurings and Struggles for Liberty were of fome Standing, when

King

King *Charles* the Firſt came to the Throne : The Jealouſies, which Parliaments had of the Regal Power and Prerogative, had been openly ſhewn in his Father's Reign, and, throughout the Courſe of it, been troubleſome to his Miniſters. That the Clergy of the Church of *England* had enjoin'd Things, and taught what they had no Warrant for from the Goſpel, and that King *James* the Firſt, as well as his Son, who ſucceeded him, laid Claim to a more abſolute Power, than was conſiſtent with the Privileges of Parliament and the Conſtitution, is undeniable. Religion then and Liberty, being Two Topicks, that Abundance was to be ſaid upon in thoſe Days, became the Subject and Foundation of the Quarrels between the King and Parliament, that afterwards broke out into a Civil War.

Hor. I was not born in *China* or *Lapland* : There is not a Boy of Twelve Years old, that is ignorant of the Cauſes of that Civil War.

Cleo. I don't queſtion your Knowledge ; but only mention theſe Things, that from the Nature of the Diſſentions, and the Miſchiefs that enſued upon them, we might ſee the Impoſſibility , that either Party ſhould have acted from a Principle of Chriſtianity.

I

I shall now endeavour to demonstrate to you Two Things ; the First is, that Clergymen, by a small Deviation from the Gospel, may so egregiously impose upon their Hearers, as to make even sincere Men act quite contrary to the Precepts of it, at the same Time that those subtle Declaimers shall seem to be full of Zeal, and to have the highest Value for Christianity. The Other is, that in a well disciplin'd Army, Acts of Devotion, and an outward Shew of Religion may do vast Service for the obtaining of Victory, tho' the General who appointed and order'd them, was an *Atheist* ; the greatest Part of the Clergy, who perform'd and assisted in them, were Hypocrites, and the Generality of the Men were wicked Livers. As to the First, I call a Man sincere in his Religion, who believes the Bible to be the Word of God, and acknowledging the Difficulty he finds in obeying the Dictates of the Gospel, wishes with all his Heart, that he could practise the Self-denial that is required in it; and is sorry, that he has not the Power to govern and subdue his stubborn Passions so well as he could wish. If to such a one, a Clergyman should preach the Strictness of Morality, and the Necessity of Repentance, that

are

are taught in the Gofpel, and moreover incul-
cate to him, that as to Divine Worſhip the
Ceremonial was abrogated; that what was required of us, was the Sacrifice of the Heart
and the Conqueſt over our darling Luſts; and
that in ſhort the Religious Duties of a Chriſtian were ſumm'd up in loving God and his
Neighbour; this Doctrine being every Way
agreeable to that of *Chriſt*, a ſincere Man, who
had read the *New Teſtament*, would eaſily give
Ear to a Divine, who ſhould preach it to him;
and it is highly probable, that in Matters of
Conſcience, and every Thing relating to his
Deportment, he ſhould be glad of his Coun-
fel. Suppofe now, that there was another
Clergyman in the fame City, who likewife
pretending to preach the Gofpel, ſhould, on
the one Hand, reprefent the Doctrine of it as
very indulging to Human Nature, and the
Practice of it eafily comply'd with, and, on the
other, lay a great Strefs on the Honour to be
paid to his own Perfon, and the Performances
of a Set of Ceremonies, no where mention'd
in the Gofpel; it is not likely, that our ſincere
Man ſhould approve of his Sermons; but if
this Second Divine ſhould moreover call them
Enemies to God, who ſhould refufe to comply

ply with every Part of thefe Ceremonies, and give the Name of Hypocrite to Every body, who fhould affert, that the Gofpel required ftricter Morality than what he taught ; if he fhould follicite the Magiftrate to have all Perfons punifh'd, who were not of his Opinion ; and if, by his Inftigation, our fincere Man fhould actually be perfecuted and plagued by his Fellow-Subjects ; to judge from what we know of Human Nature, fuch Ufage would fill the fincere Man with Indignation, and raife his Anger againft all thofe, who were the Occafion of his Sufferings. Let us fuppofe likewife, that this Man, befides his Sincerity, had Temper and Goodnefs enough to confider, that, tho' he had been unjuftly dealt with, and was highly provok'd, yet his Religion taught and commanded him not to refent Injuries, but to forgive his Enemies, and to Love them that hated him ; it is reafonable to think, that this Clafhing between Nature and Principle would perplex him, and himfelf ftand in Need of good Advice, what to do in this Dilemma. If in this Cafe, the Clergyman, who firft preached to him the Purity of the Chriftian Religion, and the Severity of its Morals, and whom he often went to hear, fhould perfift in the

fame

fame Sentiments; and, continuing to recommend to him the Doctrine of Peace, make Ufe of all the Arguments, which the Gofpel could furnifh him with, either to warn him againft Anger and all finful Paffions, Malice of Heart, Hatred and Refentment; or to exhort him to Fortitude in Afflictions, Heroick Patience in Sufferings, and on all Emergencies an entire Refignation to the Will of God; If, I fay, the Clergyman I mention'd fhould do this, whatever might be the Succefs he did it with, he would have acted the good Shepherd, and his Sermons could never be made a Handle of for War or Rebellion. But if inftead of it, he fhould feem to approve of the other's Anger, and, to juftify it, enter into the Merits of the Caufe; if he fhould endeavour to demonftrate, that all Ceremonies of Human Invention were fuperftitious, and that Kneeling down, where there were Pictures and Sculpture, was a manifeft Token of Idolatry; if after this, by an eafy Tranfition, he fhould go over to the *Old Teftament*, expatiate on the Second Commandment, and produce feveral Inftances of God's Vengeance on Idolaters, and the utter Deftruction, that had often been brought upon them by God's own People, fighting

fighting under his Banner, and acting by his special Commiſſion ; If a Preacher ſhould do this, and have Miſchief in his Heart, it would not be difficult for him inſenſibly to miſlead his Hearers, extinguiſh their Charity, and, working upon the Paſſions, make a ſincere Man, who had really been ill treated, miſtake in his own Breaſt the Spirit of Revenge for Religious Zeal, and, to maintain the Truth of the Goſpel, act directly contrary to the Precepts of it. And the more regular the Life was of ſuch a Divine, and the greater the Auſterity of his Manners, the fitter Inſtrument would he be to ſow Sedition, enflame an Audience, and make Tools of them for the Ambitious.

Hor. The Firſt you have made out beyond my Expectation ; but it has been at the Expence of your Revolution-Principles ; I hope you'll never take them up again.

Cleo. I hope I ſhall have no Occaſion for it: but what I have advanced has Nothing to do with the Controverſy you point at. The illegal Sway of Magiſtrates is not to be juſtified from the Goſpel, any more than the Reſiſtance of the People. Where Two Parties quarrel, and open Animoſities are to be ſeen on both Sides, it is ridiculous for either to appeal to the Gospel. The Right, which Princes have to enjoy their Prerogative, is not more divine, than that which Subjects have to enjoy their Privileges; and if Tyrants will think themselves more justifiable before God than Rebels, they ought first to be satisfied, that Oppression is less heinous in his Sight than Revenge.

Hor. But No body owns himself to be a Tyrant.

Cleo. Nor did ever any Malecontents own themselves to be Rebels.

Hor. I can't give this up, and must talk with you about it another Time. But now I long to hear you demonstrate the Second of your Assertions, and make that as evident to me, as you have done the First.

Cleo. I'll endeavour it, if you'll give me Leave, and can have but Patience to hear me, for you'll stand in Need of it.

Hor. You are to prove, that Acts of Devotion, and an outward Shew of Religion, may make an Army Victorious, tho' the General was an *Atheist*, the Clergy were Hypocrites, and the Generality of the Men wicked Livers.

Cleo. A little more Accuracy, if you please.

I

I said, that they might do vaſt Service for the obtaining of Victory; the Service I mean, conſiſts in rouſing the Courage of the Men, and throwing them into an Enthuſiaſm, that ſhall diſſipate their Fears, and make them deſpiſe the greateſt Dangers. There is no greater Art to make Men fight with Obſtinacy, than to make them truſt to, and rely with Confidence on the Aſſiſtance of the inviſible Cauſe, they Fear.

Hor. But how can wicked Men be made to do this? What Reaſons can they be furniſh'd with, to hope for the Aſſiſtance of Heaven?

Cleo. If you can aſſure Men of the Juſtice of their Cauſe, and render that evident and unqueſtionable, the Buſineſs is done, and their own Wickedneſs will be no Obſtacle to it. Therefore this, you ſee, is the Grand Point, which Prieſts have ever labour'd to gain among Fighting Men in all Countries and in all Ages. How immenſely ſoever they have differ'd from one another in Religion and Worſhip, in this they have all agreed. We were ſpeaking, you know, of *Cromwell*'s Army; do but recollect what you have heard and read of thoſe Times, and you'll find, that the Notions and Sentiments, that were in‐

duſtriouſly

duftrioufly inftill'd into the Minds of the Soldiers, had a manifeft Tendency to obtain this End, and that all their Preaching and Praying were made ferviceable to the fame Purpofe. The *Credenda*, which the whole Army, and every Individual were imbued with, even by the moft moderate of their Preachers, were generally thefe: That the King gave Ear to evil Counfellours; that he was govern'd by his Queen, who was a rank Papift, bigotted to her own Superftition; that all his Minifters were wicked Men, who endeavour'd to fubvert the Conftitution, and aim'd at Nothing more than to render him abfolute, that by his Arbitrary Power they might be fkreen'd from Juftice, and the Refentment of an injured Nation: That the Bifhops were in the fame Intereft; that, tho' they had abjured the Pope's Supremacy, and found Fault with the Luxury of the Court of *Rome*, they wanted as much to lord it over the Laity themfelves, and were as fond of worldly Honour, Power, and Authority, of Pomp and Splendour, and a diftinguifh'd Manner of Living, as any Popifh Prelates: That the Worfhip of the Church of *England* was above half Popery; that moft of the Clergy were idle Drones, who lived upon the

the Fat of the Land, and perverted the End of their Function : That by this Means Religion it self was neglected, and, instead of it, Rights and Ceremonies were obstinately insisted upon, that were notoriously borrow'd from the Heathen and Jewish Priests. That preaching Non-resistance was justifying Tyranny, and could have no other Meaning than to encourage Princes to be wicked, and tie the Peoples Hands, whilst they should have their Throats cut : That in Pursuance of this Doctrine, He, who should have been the Guardian of their Laws, had already trampled upon them and broken his Coronation-Oath, and, instead of being a Father to his People, had openly proclaim'd himself their Enemy, invited a Foreign Force into the Land, and was now actually making War against the Parliament, the undoubted Representatives of the Nation. Whilst these Things were said of the Adverse Party, their own was extoll'd to the Skies ; and loud Encomiums were made on the Patriotism of their Superiours, the Sanctity and Disinterestedness as well as Wisdom and Capacity of those Asserters of Liberty, who had rescued them from Bondage. Sometimes they spoke of the Care, that was taken of Religion,

and

and a Pains-taking Miniſtry, that preach'd not themſelves but *Chriſt*, and, by their Example as well as Precept, taught the Purity of the Goſpel, and the ſtrict Morality that is contain'd in it, without Superſtition or Allowances to pleaſe Sinners : At others, they repreſented to their Hearers the exemplary Lives of the Generals, the Sobriety of the Soldiers, and the Goodneſs and Piety, as well as Zeal and Heroiſm of the whole Army.

Hor. But what is all this to what you was to prove? I want to know the vaſt Service an outward Shew of Religion can be of to wicked Men, for the obtaining of Victory : When ſhall I ſee that?

Cleo. Preſently; but you muſt give me Leave to prove it my own Way. In what I have ſaid hitherto, I have only laid before you the Artifice, which Every body knows was made Uſe of by the *Roundheads* in haranguing their own Troops, to render the *Cavaliers* and the King's Cauſe odious and deteſtable to them on the one Hand, and to make them, on the other, have an high Opinion of their own, and firmly believe, that God could not but favour it. Now let us call to Mind the Situation of Affairs in the Times I ſpeak of, and the Politicks

ticks of thofe, who oppofed the King, and
then confider, what a crafty defigning General ought to have done to make the moft of
the Conjuncture he lived in, and the Zeal and
Spirit that were then reigning among the Party he was engaged in; if he had Nothing at
Heart, but to advance, *per fas aut nefas,* his
own worldly Intereft and his own Glory : In
the Firft Place, it would never have been believed that the *Prefbyters* were in Earneft,
who found Fault with and rail'd at the Luxury and loofe Morals, as well as Lazinefs of
the National Clergy, if they had not been
more diligent in their Calling, and led ftricter
Lives themfelves. This therefore was com-
plied with, and the diffenting Clergy took vaft
Pains in Praying and Preaching without Book
for Hours together, and practis'd much greater Self-denial, at leaft to outward Appearance,
than their Adverfaries. The Laity of the fame
Side, to compafs their End, were obliged to
follow the Example of their Teachers in Severity of Manners, and Pretences to Religion :
Accordingly they did, at leaft well enough, you
fee, to acquire the Name of the Sober Party.

Hor. Then you muft think, that they had
none but Hypocrites among them.

Cleo.

Cleo. Indeed I don't; but I believe, that moſt of the Ring-leaders who began the Quarrel with the King had Temporal Advantages in View, or other private Ends to ſerve, that had no Relation either to the Service of God or the Welfare of the People; and yet I believe likewiſe, that many ſincere and well-meaning Men were drawn into their Meaſures. When a Reformation of Manners is once ſet on Foot, and ſtrict Morality is well ſpoken of, and countenanc'd by the better Sort of People, the very Faſhion will make Proſelytes to Virtue. Swearing and not Swearing in Converſation depend upon Mode and Cuſtom. Nothing is more reaſonable, than Temperance and Honeſty to Men that conſult their Health and their Intereſt; where Men are not debarr'd from Marriage, Chaſtity is eaſily comply'd with, and prevents a Thouſand Miſchiefs. There is Nothing more univerſal than the Love of Liberty; and there is Something engaging in the Sound of the Words. The Love of one's Country is natural; and very bad Men may feel it as warm about them, as very good Men; and it is a Principle, which a Man may as ſincerely act from, who Fights againſt his King, as he who Fights for him. But theſe ſincere and

well-

well-meaning People, that can pray and fight, sing Pfalms and do Mifchief with a good Confcience, may in many Refpects be Morally good, and yet want moft of the Virtues, that are peculiar to Chriftianity, and, if the Gofpel fpeaks Truth, neceffary to Salvation. A Man may be continent and likewife never drink to Excefs, and yet be haughty and infupportable in his Carriage, a litigious Neighbour, an unnatural Father, and a barbarous Hufband. He may be juft in his Dealings, and wrong No body in his Property, yet he may be full of Envy, take Delight in Slander, be revengeful in his Heart, and never known to have forgiven an Injury. He may abftain from Curfing and all idle as well as prophane Swearing, and at the fame Time be uncharitable and wifh Evil to all, that are not of his Opinion ; nay, he may mortally hate, and take Pleafure in perfecuting and doing Mifchief to, all thofe who differ from him in Religion.

Hor. I fee plainly now, how Men may be fincere in their Religion, and by Art be made to act quite contrary to the Precepts of it : And your Manner of accounting for this, does not only render the Sober Party lefs odious, than the Orthodox have reprefented them ; but

but there is likewife greater Probability in it,
than there is in what they generally fay of them:
For that an Army of a great many Thoufand
Men fhould confift of None but Hypocrites,
who yet fhould fight well, is an inconceivable
Thing. But what is it you would fay of the
General ?

Cleo. I would fhew you, how an obfcure
Man, of an active Spirit and boundlefs Ambition, might raife himfelf among fuch a Set of
People to the higheft Poft; and having once
got the Supreme Command of the Army,
what Method, and what Arts it is moft probable he would make Ufe of to model fuch
Troops to his Purpofe, and make them ferviceable to the Advancement of his own Greatnefs.

Hor. But remember he muft be an *Atheift.*

Cleo. He fhall be fo, in the Vulgar Accepta-
tion of the Word; that is, he fhall have no
Religion or Confcience; fear neither God nor
Devil, and not believe either a Providence in
this World, or any Thing that is faid of another: But he muft be a great Genius, daring to
the higheft Degree, indefatigable, fupple to his
Intereft, and ready as well as capable to act any
Part, and put on any Difguife, that fhall be re-
qui-

quired to ferve or promote it. Every brifk, forward Man, who pretends to an extraordinary Zeal for his Party, and the Caufe he is engaged in, and who fhews Eagernefs for Action, and behaves with Intrepidity in Danger, cannot remain long unknown, where Men have frequent Opportunities of fignalizing themfelves. But if he be likewife a Man of Senfe, who underftands his Bufinefs, and has Conduct as well as Courage, he can't fail of Preferment in an Army, where the Intereft of the common Caufe is taken Care of. If he ferves among *Puritans*, who pretend to a ftricter Morality, and to be more religious than their Neighbours, and himfelf is an artful Man, as foon as he is taken Notice of, he'll fall in with the Cant in Fafhion, talk of Grace and Regeneration, counterfeit Piety, and feem to be fincerely Devout. If he can do this well, put on a fanctify'd Face, and abftain from being openly vicious, it is incredible what Luftre it will add to the Reft of his Qualifications, in fuch a Conjuncture : And if moreover he is a Man of Addrefs, and can get the Reputation of being difinterefted and a Soldier's Friend, in a fhort Time he'll become the Darling of the Army; and it would

hardly

hardly be fafe long to deny him any Poft, he can reafonably pretend to. In all Wars, where the contending Parties are in good Earneft, and the Animofities between them run high, Campaigns are always active, and many brave Men muft fall on both Sides; and where there fhould be much Room for Advancement, it is highly probable, that fuch a Man as I have de-fcrib'd, if at his firft fetting out he was Cap-tain of Horfe, and had raifed an entire Troop at his own Charge, fhould in a few Years come to be a General Officer, and of great Weight in all Councils and Debates. Being thus far preferr'd, if he would make the moft of his Talents, he might be of infinite Service to his Party. An afpiring Man, whofe grand Aim was to thrive by Hypocrify, would ftudy the Scripture, learn the Language of it, and occafionally mix it with his Difcourfe. He would cajole the Clergy of his Party, and of-ten do good Offices to thofe of them that were moft popular. A Man of his Parts would preach *ex tempore* himfelf, and get the Knack of Praying for as many Hours as there fhould be Occafion. Whoever is well fkill'd in thefe Exercifes may counterfeit Enthufiafm when he pleafes, and pretend on fome Emergencies

to

to receive Directions from God himself; and that he is manifestly influenc'd by his Spirit. A General Officer, who has once got this Reputation, may carry almost any Thing; for Few that are wise will venture to oppose what such a Man, pretending to have sought the Lord, declares to be his Opinion. Whatever Victories might be obtain'd, and in all Successes under his Command, a skilful Hypocrite would make a Shew of Modesty, refuse to hear the Praises that are his due, and seem with great Humility to give all the Glory to God only; not forgetting, at the same Time, to flatter the Pride of his Troops, highly to commend and magnify, first the Goodness and Bravery of the Soldiers, and then the Care and Vigilance of the Officers under him. To be well serv'd, he would reward Merit, punish and discountenance Vice, always speak well and magnificently of Virtue, and seem to be just himself. But as to Christianity it self, he would not suffer any Thing to be taught of it, that could interfere with the Principle of Honour, or any of the Artifices to keep up the Ill Will, and Hatred which military Men are to be inspired with against their Enemies. The Christian Duties, which he would chiefly

take

take Care of and see perform'd, would be outward Acts of Devotion, and that Part of Religion which is easily comply'd with, and yet taken Notice of by all the World; such as frequent Prayers, long and pathetick Sermons, singing of Psalms, and the keeping of the Sabbath with great Strictness; all which Men may assist at and employ themselves in, tho' their Hearts are otherwise engag'd. It is certain, that a Man of vast Parts and superlative Ambition might, by the Divine Permission, perform, take Care of, and compass all this, tho' he was an *Atheist*; and that he might live and die with the Reputation of a Saint, if he was but circumspect and wise enough to conceal himself so entirely well, that no Penetration or Watchfulness of Mortals could ever discover his real Sentiments. There is no Atchievement to be expected from Soldiers, which they would not perform for such a General; and his Name would be sufficient to fill the greatest Profligate in an Army with a Religious Enthusiasm, if he disbelieved not an invisible Cause.

Hor. There lies the Difficulty; it is that which I cannot comprehend.

Cleo. Wickedness, I have hinted to you before, is no Bar to Superstition; and a great
Pro-

184 *The Third Dialogue.*

Profligate may at the fame Time be a filly Fellow, believe Abfurdities, and rely on Trifles, which a Man of Senfe and Virtue could not be influenc'd or affected by. It is eafily imagin'd, that in fuch an Army, under fuch a General as I have been fpeaking of, the Men would be kept under ftrict Difcipline; and that they would not only be compell'd, whether they would or not, to affift at all their Exercifes of outward Devotion and Publick Worfhip; but likewife that the loofeft Livers among them fhould be obliged to be more cautious and circumfpect in their Behaviour, than Soldiers generally are. Now fuppofe a Man fo wicked, that, tho' he has no Doubt of a Future State, the Belief of Rewards and Punifhments in another World made no Impreffion upon him; but that he indulged every vicious Inclination as far as he dared, lay with every Woman that would let him, and got drunk as often as he could get an Opportunity to do it; one that would ftick at Nothing, rob or fteal, kill a Man that fhould anger him, if he was not with-held by the Law, and the Fear of Temporal Punifhment: Suppofe likewife, that this was one of the loweft Mob, who being in Want, and too lazy to

work

work, fhould lift himfelf in fome Regiment or other of this Army. There is no Doubt. but this Man would be forc'd immediately to have a greater Guard upon his Actions, and reform, at leaft outwardly, more than would fuit with his Inclinations, and therefore it is not unlikely, that, what Duties foever he might comply with, and whatever Appearance he might make among the Reft, in his Heart he fhould remain the fame he was before. Yet notwithftanding all this, in a little Time he might make a very good Soldier. I can eafily conceive, how the Wearing of a Sword and Regimental Cloaths, and always converfing with refolute and well difciplin'd Men, among whom Arms and Gallantry are in the higheft Efteem, might fo far encreafe a wicked Fellow's Pride, that he fhould wifh to be brave, and in a few Months think Nothing more really dreadful, than to be thought a Coward. The Fear of Shame may act as powerfully upon bad Men, as it can upon good ; and the Wickednefs of his Heart would not hinder him from having a good Opinion of himfelf, and the Caufe he ferved ; nor yet from hating his Enemies or taking Delight in deftroying, plundering, and doing all Manner of Mifchief.   *Hor.*

Hor. But having no Regard to Godlinefs or Religion, it is impoffible, that he fhould be influenc'd or affected by the Prayers or other Exercifes of Devotion, which he might affift at and which, in all Probability, he would never come near, unlefs he was compell'd to it.

Cleo. I don't fuppofe, that he would be influenced or affected by them at all himfelf; but he might eafily believe, that others were. I take it for granted, that in fuch an Army there might have been Abundance of well-meaning Men, that were really honeft, and fincere in their Religion, tho' they had been mifled in what concern'd the Duties of it. From the Behaviour of thefe, and the Imitation of others, from the Exemplary Lives, which our Reprobate fhould fee among them, and the eftablifh'd Reputation of fo many Men of Honour, he would have all the Reafon in the World to think, that at leaft the greateft Part of them were in good Earneft; that they relied upon God; and that the fervent Zeal, with which they feem'd to implore his Affiftance, was real and unfeign'd. All wicked Men are not inflexible; and there are great Sinners, whom this Confideration would move to the quick; and tho' perhaps it would not be of

Force

Force enough to reclaim them, there are many, who, by Means of it, would be made to relent, and wish that they were better. But I don't want this Help ; and we'll suppose our Profligate such a stubborn Wretch, and so obstinately vicious, that the most moving Discourses, and the most fervent Prayers, tho' he is forc'd to assist at them, have not the least Power to make him reflect either on his Sins or his Duty ; and that notwithstanding what he hears and sees of others, his Heart remains as bad as ever, and himself as immoral as he dares to be for Fear of his Officers. We'll suppose, I say, all this; but as it is taken for granted, that he believes the World to be govern'd by Providence ——.

Hor. But why should that be taken for granted, of a Fellow so thoroughly wicked?

Cleo. Because it is included in his Belief of a Future State, which, in his Character, I supposed him not to doubt of.

Hor. I know it ; but what Reason had you to suppose this at First, in a Man who never gave any Signs, nor ever did insinuate, for ought you know, that he had such a Belief?

Cleo. Because he never gave any Signs to the Contrary ; and in a Christian Country,

I

I fuppofe all Men to believe the Exiftence of a God and a Future State, who, by fpeaking or writing, never declared, that they did not. Wickednefs confifting in an unreafonable Gratification of every Paffion that comes uppermoft, it is fo far from implying Unbelief, or what is call'd Atheifm, that it rather excludes it. Becaufe the Fear of an invifible Caufe is as much a Paffion in our Nature, as the Fear of Death. I have hinted to you before, that great Cowards, whilft they are in Health and Safety, may live many Years without difcovering the leaft Symptom of the Fear of Death, fo as to be vifibly affected by it; but that this is no Sign, that they have it not, is evident when they are in Danger. It is the fame with the Fear of an invifible Caufe; the one is as much born with us as the other, and to conquer either, is more difficult than is eafily imagin'd. The Fear of an invifible Caufe is univerfal, how widely foever Men may differ in the Worfhip of it; and it was never obferved among a Multitude, that the worft were more backward than the beft in believing whatever from their Infancy they had heard concerning this invifible Caufe; how abfurd or fhocking foever that might have been. The
moft

moſt Wicked are often the moſt Superſtitious, and as ready as any to believe Witchcraft, conſult Fortune-tellers, and make Uſe of Charms. And tho' among the moſt brutiſh Part of the Mob, we ſhould meet with Some, that neither pray nor pay Worſhip to any Thing, laugh at Things ſacred, and openly diſclaim all Religion, we could have no Reaſon to think, even from theſe, that they acted from Principles of Infidelity, when from their Behaviour and many of their Actions, it ſhould be manifeſt, that they apprehended Something or other, that could do them Good or Hurt, and yet is inviſible. But as to the vileſt Reprobates among the Vulgar, from their very Curſes and the moſt prophane of their Oaths and Imprecations, it is plain, that they are Believers.

Hor. That's far fetch'd.

Cleo. I don't think ſo. Can a Man wiſh himſelf damn'd, without ſuppoſing, that there is ſuch a Thing as Damnation. Believe me, *Horatio*, there are no *Atheiſts* among the Common People: You never knew any of them entirely free from Superſtition, which always implies Belief: And whoever lays any Streſs upon Predictions, upon good or bad Omens; or does but think, that ſome Things are lucky and

and others unlucky, muſt believe, that there is
an over-ruling Power, which meddles with,
and interferes in Human Affairs.

Hor. I muſt yield this to you, I think.

Cleo. If then our wicked, obdurate Soldier
believes, that there is a God, and that the
World is govern'd by Providence, it is impoſſible, when Two Armies are to engage, but
he muſt think, that it is very material, and a
Thing of the higheſt Importance, which of
them God will be pleas'd to favour, and wiſh
with all his Heart, that Heaven would be of
his Side. Now, if he knows that the Troops,
he ſerves among, have gain'd ſeveral Advantages over their Enemies, and that he has been
an Eye-witneſs of this himſelf, he muſt ne-
ceſſarily think, that God has a greater Regard
to them, than he has to thoſe that are beaten
by them. It is certain, that a Man, who is
ſtrongly perſuaded of this, will be more undaunted, and with the ſame Degree of Skill,
Malice and Strength, fight better than he
could do, if he believ'd the Contrary. It is
evident then, that the moſt abandon'd Raſcal
in a Chriſtian Army may be made a valuable
Man on the Score of Fighting, as ſoon as he
can be perſuaded, that God takes his Part, tho'

he

he never made any further Reflection: But it
is inconceivable, that a Man fhould firmly believe what I have faid without reflecting one
Time or other on what might be the Caufe
of this particular Favour, this vifible Affiftance of Heaven; and if ever he did, could he
help thinking on the Preaching and Praying,
which he was daily prefent at; and would he
not be forced from all the Circumftances to
believe, that thofe Things were acceptable to
God; and conclude upon the whole, that thofe
Religious Exercifes were a proper Means to
obtain God's Friendfhip? Would he not be
very much confirm'd in this Opinion, if he
faw or but heard of credible People, that, in
the Enemy's Army, the Men were more cold
and remifs in their Worfhip, or at leaft, that
they made a lefs outward Shew of Devotion,
which is all that he fhould be able ro judge by?

Hor. But why fhould you think, that fuch
an abandon'd, obdurate Fellow, as you have
fuppofed him to be, fhould ever trouble his
Head with the Difference in Worfhip between
one Army and another, or ever think at all on
any Thing relating to Devotion?

Cleo. Becaufe it would be impoffible for
him to help it. I have not fuppofed, that he
was

was either Deaf or Blind: The Things I named, and which I imagin'd he would be forc'd
to believe, would be rung in his Ears, and
repeated to him over and over from every
Quarter: The Soldiers would be full of them;
the Officers would talk of them. He would
be prefent at the folemn Thanksgivings, they
paid to Heaven. The Preachers would often
be loud in commending the Godlinefs as well
as Bravery of the Army, and roar out the Prai-
fes of their General, that fanctify'd Veffel,
whom they would call a *Gideon*, a *Joshua*, a
Mofes, that glorious Inftrument, which God
had raifed and made Ufe of to refcue his
Church from Idolatry and Superftition, and
his Saints from Tyranny and Oppreffion. They
would exclaim againft the Wickednefs and
Immorality of their Enemies, inveigh againft
Lawn-Sleeves and Surplices, Altar-Pieces, and
Common-Prayers; call the Orthodox Clergy,
the Priefts of *Baal*, and affure their Hearers,
that the Lord hated the *Cavaliers*; that they
were an Abomination to him, and that he
would certainly deliver them into the Hands
of his chofen People. When a Man is obliged to hear all this, and fees moreover the
Spirit and Alacrity that is raifed in his Comrades

rades after a moving extemporary Prayer, the real Enthufiafm the Men are thrown into by the Singing of a Pfalm, and the Tears of Zeal and Joy run down the Cheeks of Men, whom he knows to be Faithful and Sincere, as well as Refolute and Daring. When a Man, I fay, fuch a one as I have defcrib'd, fhould be forc'd to hear and fee all this, it would hardly be poffible for him, not to believe, in the firft Place, that God actually affifted this Army; and in the Second, that the Means, by which that Affiftance was procured, were the Strictnefs of the Difcipline and the Religious Duties, that were obferved in it; tho' he himfelf fhould never Join in the one, or Submit to the other, but againft his Will, and with the utmoft Reluctancy. I am perfuaded, that fuch an Opinion, well rivetted in a Man, would, in fuch an Army as I am fpeaking of, be of vaft Ufe to him in all Adventures and Expeditions of War; and that, if he was fit at all to be made a Soldier, it would in the Day of Battle infpire him with a Confidence and Undauntednefs, which the fame Man could never have acquired, *Cæteris Paribus*, if he had ferved among other Troops, where Divine Worfhip had been little infifted upon, or but flightly

per-

perform'd. And if this be true, I have proved to you, that Acts of Devotion, and an outward Shew of Re'igion, may be serviceable to the greatest Profligate for the obtaining of Victory, tho' the General should be an *Atheist*, most of the Clergy Hypocrites, and the greatest Part of the Army wicked Men.

Hor. I can see very well the Possibility, that a few Profligates, among a great many others, that were not so, might be kept in Awe by strict Discipline, and that Acts of Devotion might be serviceable even to those, who were present at them against their Wills. But this Possibility is only built upon a Supposition, that the Rest of the Army should be better disposed: For if the Generality of them were not in Earnest, you could have no outward Shew of Religion; and the Things which you say the obdurate wretch should be forced to hear and see, could have no Existence. No Preaching or Praying can be moving to those, that are harden'd and inattentive; and no Man can be thrown into an Enthusiasm upon the Singing of Psalms, and shed Tears of Zeal and Joy in any Part of Divine Worship, unless they give Heed to it, and are really Devout.

Cleo

Cleo. I am glad you ftart this Objection ; for it puts me in Mind of Something, that will ferve to illuftrate this whole Matter, and which, if you had not mention'd this, I fhould have had no Opportunity to fpeak of. I took for granted, you know, that in the Quarrel between the King and the People, there had been many honeft well meaningMen, among the Sober Party, that by Artifice were drawn into the Meafures of cunning Hypocrites, who, under fpecious Pretences, carried on the Rebellion with no other View than their own Advantage. But if you recollect what I faid then, you'll find, that many of thofe honeft well-meaning Men might have been very bad Chriftians. A Man may be a fair Dealer, and wifh well to his Country, and yet be very wicked in many other Refpects. But whatever Vices he may be guilty of, if he believes the Scriptures without Referve, is forry for his Sins, and fometimes really afraid, that he fhall be punifh'd for them in another World, he is certainly fincere in his Religion, tho' he never mends. Some of the moft wicked in the World have been great Believers. Confider all the Money, that has been given to pray Souls out of Purgatory, and who
they

they were, that left the greateſt Legacies to
the Church. The Generality of Mankind believe what they were taught in their Youth,
let that be what it will, and there is no Superſtition ſo groſs or abſurd, nor any Thing ſo
improbable or contradictory in any Religion,
but Men may be ſincere in the Belief of it.
What I ſay all this for is to ſhew you, that an
honeſt well-meaning Man may believe the
Bible and be ſincere in his Religion, when
he is yet very remote from being a good Chriſtian. What I underſtand then by Sincere is
evident: Now give me Leave to tell you what
I mean by Wicked, and to put you in Mind of
what I have ſaid of it already; *viz.* that I gave
that Name to thoſe, *who indulge their Paſſions
as they come uppermoſt, without Regard to the
Good or Hurt, which the Gratification of their
Appetites may do to the Society.* But all wicked Men are not equally neglectful of Religious
Duties, nor equally inflexible; and you won't
meet with one in a Hundred ſo ſtubborn and
averſe to all Senſe of Divine Worſhip, as I
have ſuppoſed our Profligate to be. My Reaſon for drawing ſo bad a Character, was to
convince you, that, if an outward Shew of
Religion could be made ſerviceable to the moſt
ſtubborn

stubborn Reprobate, it could never fail of having a good Effect upon all others, that should be more relenting, and assist at it with less Reluctancy. Few Men are wicked for Want of good Will to be better: The greatest Villains have Remorses; and hardly any of them are so bad, that the Fear of an invisible Cause and future Punishment should never make any Impression upon them; if not in Health, at least in Sickness. If we look narrowly into the Sentiments, as well as Actions even of those that persist in evil Courses for many Years, and spend their whole Lives in Debaucheries, we shall hardly ever find, that it is because they are obstinately bent to be Wicked; but because they want either the Power to govern their Passions, or else the Resolution to set about it; that they have often wish'd, that they could lead better Lives; that they hope, God will forgive them; and that several Times they have fix'd a Time for their Repentance, but that always Something or other interven'd, that has hinder'd them, till at last they died without having ever met with the Opportunity they wish'd for. Such Men as these perhaps would never go to Prayers, or to hear a Sermon as long as they lived, if they could

help

help it : But moſt of them, if they were forc'd
to it, would behave very well, and actually
receive Benefit from being there ; eſpecially in
Armies,where Nothing being leſs wanted than
contrite Hearts and broken Spirits, Nothing is
mention'd that is mortifying, or would depreſs the Mind ; and if ever any thing melancholy is ſlightly touch'd upon, it is done with
great Art, and only to make a Contraſt with
Something reviving, that is immediately to
follow, which will flatter their Pride, and
make them highly delighted with themſelves.
All Exhortations to Battle ſhould be chearful
and pleaſing. What is required of the Men,
is, that they ſhould Fight undauntedly and
obſtinately.   Therefore all Arts are made uſe
of to raiſe and keep up their Spirits on the one
Hand, and their Hatred to their Enemies on
the other.   To diſſipate their Fears, they are
aſſured of the Juſtice and Goodneſs of their
Cauſe, that God himſelf is engaged, and his
Honour concern'd in it ; and that therefore, if
they can but ſhew Zeal enough for him,and are
not wanting to themſelves, they need not
doubt of the Victory.

Hor. It is amazing, that Believers, who are
ſo conſcious of their own Wickedneſs, ſhould
be

be fo eafily perfuaded, that God would do any Thing in their Favour.

Cleo. The great Propenfity we have in our Nature to flatter our felves, makes us eafy Cafuifts in our own Concerns. Every body knows, that God is merciful, and that all Men are Sinners. The Thought of this has often been a great Comfort to very bad Livers, efpecially if they could remember, that ever they wifh'd to be better ; which, among Believers, there is not One in a Hundred, but can. This good Difpofition of Mind a wicked Man may make a notable Conftruction of, and magnify the Merit of it, till the Reflection of it is fufficient to make his Confcience eafy, and he abfolves himfelf without the Trouble of Repentance. I can eafily conceive, how one of the Vulgar, no better qualify'd, may affift at Publick Worfhip with Satisfaction, and even Pleafure ; if Preaching and Praying are managed in the Manner I have hinted at : And it is not difficult to imagine, how by a little paultry Eloquence, and Violence of Geftures, a Man in this Situation may be hurried away from his Reafon, and have his Paffions fo artfully play'd upon ; that feeling himfelf thoroughly moved, he fhall miftake the Malice

lice of his Heart, and perhaps the Resentment of a great Wound received, for the Love of God and Zeal for Religion. There is another Class of wicked Men, that I have not touch'd upon yet ; and of which there would always be great Numbers among such Troops as we have been speaking of, *viz.* Soldiers of the Sober Party, where Swearing, Prophaneness, and all open Immorality are actually punish'd; where a grave Deportment and strict Behaviour are encouraged, and where Scripture-Language and Pretences to Holiness are in Fashion ; in an Army of which the General is firmly believed to be a Saint, and acts his part to Admiration.

Hor. It is reasonable to think, I own, that in such an Army, to one sincere Man, there would always be three or four Hypocrites ; for these I suppose are the Class you mean.

Cleo. They are so. And considering, that, to save Appearances, Hypocrites are at least as good as the sincere Men I have spoken of, it is impossible, that there should not be a great Shew of Religion among them, if there were but eight or ten of them sincere in every Hundred : And where such Pains should be taken to make the Men seem to be Godly ; and this

Point

Point of outward Worſhip ſhould be labour'd
with ſo much Diligence and Aſſiduity, I am
perſuaded, that many even of thoſe, who
ſhould be too wicked to be Hypocrites, and to
counterfeit long, would ſometimes, not only
pray in good Earneſt, but likewiſe, ſet on by
the Examples before them, be tranſported
with real Zeal for the Good of their Cauſe.

Hor. There is no Doubt but Enthuſiaſm
among a Multitude is as catching as Yawning:
But I don't underſtand very well what you
mean by too wicked to be Hypocrites; for I
look upon them to be the worſt of all Men.

Cleo. I am very glad you named this.
There are two Sorts of Hypocrites, that
differ very much from one another. To
diſtinguiſh them by Names, the One I would
call the Malicious, and the Other the Faſhion-
able. By malicious Hypocrites, I mean Such
as pretend to a great Deal of Religion, when
they know their Pretenſions to be falſe; who
take Pains to appear Pious and Devout, in order
to be Villains, and in Hopes that they ſhall be
truſted to get an Opportunity of deceiving
thoſe, who believe them to be ſincere. Faſh-
ionable Hypocrites I call thoſe, who, without
any Motive of Religion, or Senſe of Duty, go to
Church,

Church, in Imitation of their Neighbours; counterfeit Devotion, and, without any Defign upon others, comply occafionally with all the Rites and Ceremonies of Publick Worfhip, from no other Principle than an Averfion to Singularity, and a Defire of being in the Fafhion. The firft are, as you fay, the worft of Men : but the other are rather beneficial to Society, and can only be injurious to themfelves.

Hor. Your Diftinction is very juft, if thefe latter deferve to be call'd Hypocrites at all.

Cleo. To make a Shew outwardly of what is not felt within, and counterfeit what is not real, is certainly Hypocrify, whether it does Good or Hurt.

Hor. Then, ftrictly fpeaking, good Manners and Politenefs muft come under the fame Denomination.

Cleo. I remember the Time you would by no Means have allow'd this.

Hor. Now, you fee I do, and freely own, that you have given me great Satisfaction this Afternoon ; only there is one Thing you faid five or fix Minutes ago, that has raifed a Difficulty which I don't know how to get over.

Cleo. What is it, pray ?

Hor. I don't think we fhall have Time ——

Cleo. Supper, I fee, is going in.   T H E

THE

Fourth Dialogue

BETWEEN

Horatio and *Cleomenes*.

Horatio.

 Am glad my little Dinner pleaſed you. I don't love large Pieces of Meat for a ſmall Company ; eſpe-cially in warm Weather : They heat the Room, and are offenſive even upon a Side-board.

Cleo. It was very handſome indeed ; and *Horatio* is elegant in every Thing. Your Fa-vours of Yeſterday, your Coming without Form, was ſo engaging, that I was reſolved to repay the Compliment without Delay.

Hor.

Hor. Aſſure your ſelf, that your Payment is not more prompt, than it is welcome.

Cleo. I know no higher Enjoyment, than that of your Friendſhip. But pray, what was the Difficulty you hinted at laſt Night, when Supper broke off our Diſcourſe?

Hor. When you ſpoke of Preaching and Praying in Armies, you ſaid, that Nothing was ever mention'd to them, that was mortifying, or would depreſs the Mind. I had heard the ſame from you in Subſtance more than once before; and I own, that the Nature of the Thing ſeems to require, that Soldiers ſhould be indulg'd in their Pride, and that all Exhortations to Battle ſhould be chearful and pleaſing. But the laſt Time you was ſpeaking of this, I recollected what I had read of the Solemn Faſts, that were ſo frequently obſerved in *Oliver*'s Days; and preſently I was puzled, and no ways able to account for the Uſefulneſs of them in War, by the Syſtem which you had made appear to be very rational. The Fact it ſelf, that *Cromwell* appointed many Days of Faſting and Humiliation, and made them be ſtrictly kept, is undeniable; but it is impoſſible, they ſhould promote Chearfulneſs; and what Purpoſe they could

could have been made to ferve, that was not religious, I can not conceive. The mechanical Effect, which Fafting can have upon the Spirits, is to lower, flatten, and deprefs them; and the very Effence of Humiliation is the Mortification of Pride. You have own'd, that *Cromwell* underftood Human Nature, and was a crafty Politician ; but you would never allow, that he had the leaft Intention of promoting Piety, or rendring his Men good Chriftians.

Cleo. The Objection you have ftarted feems to be of great Weight at firft View ; but if we look more narrowly into it, and examine this Affair, as we have done fome other Things, the Difficulty you labour under will foon difappear. From the Nature of Man and Society it muft follow, that whatever particular Vices may be more or lefs predominant in different Climates and different Ages, Luxury and Pride will always be reigning Sins in all civiliz'd Nations : Againft thefe two ftubborn, and always epidemic Maladies, the great Phyfician of the Soul has, in his Gofpel Difpenfation, left us two fovereign Remedies, Fafting and Humiliation; which, when rightly ufed, and duely affifted with the Exercife of Prayer, never fail to cure the Difeafes I named in the moft

def

defperate Cafes. No Method likewife is more reafonable; for, tho' *Jesus Christ* had not recommended it himfelf, it is impoffible to think on any Prefcription, more judicioufly adapted to an Ailment, than Fafting and Humiliation, accompany'd with fervent Prayer, are to Luxury and Pride. This is the Reafon, that in private as well as public Difafters, and all Adverfities in which it was thought that the divine Anger was vifible, all Believers in *Christ* have, ever fince the Promulgation of the Gofpel, made ufe of the aforefaid Remedies, as the moft proper Means to obtain Pardon for their Offences, and render Heaven propitious to them. All Magiftrates likewife, where the Chriftian Religion has been national, have in general Misfortunes and all great Calamities (whenever they happen'd) appointed Days to be folemnly kept, and fet afide for Prayer, for Fafting and Humiliation. If on thefe Days Men fhould be fincere in their Devotion; if a pains-taking Clergy, of Apoftolic Lives, on the one Hand, fhould preach Repentance to their Hearers, and fhew them the Difference between the temporal Evils, which they complain'd of, tho' they were lefs afflicting than they had deferv'd, and the eternal Miferies, which
impe-

impenitent Sinners would unavoidably meet
with, tho' now they thought little of them ;
if the Hearers, on the other, fearching their Confciences without Referve, fhould reflect upon
their paft Conduct ; if both the Clergy and the
Laity fhould thus join in religious Exercifes, and, adding real Fafting to ardent Prayer,
humble themfelves before the Throne of Mercy, with Sorrow and Contrition ; if, I fay, the
Days you fpeak of were to be fpent in this
Manner, they could be of ufe in no War, but
againft the World, the Flefh, or the Devil,
the only Enemies a Chriftian Hero is not oblig'd to love, and over which the Triumph is
the darling Object of his Ambition, and the
glorious End of his Warfare. On the Contrary, fuch Faft-days would be hurtful to a
Soldier, in the literal Senfe of the Word, and
deftructive to the Intentions of all Armies ;
and I would as foon expect from them, that
they fhould turn Men into Trees or Stones, as
that they fhould infpire them with martial
Courage, or make them eager to fight. But
skilful Politicians make an Advantage of every
Thing, and often turn into ufeful Tools the
feeming Obftacles to their Ambition. The
moft

moft refolute Unbeliever, if he is a good Hypocrite, may pretend to as much Superftition
and holy Fear, as the moft timorous Bigot can
be really poffefs'd with ; and the Firft often
gains his Point by making ufe of the Religion
of others, where the Latter is undone by being
hamper'd with his own.

Hor. This was very evident in *Oliver Cromwel* and King *James* the Second. But what
would you infer from it in Relation to Faft-
Days ?

Cleo. The moft facred Inftitutions of Chri-
ftianity may, by the Affiftance of pliable Di-
vines, be made ferviceable to the moft anti-
chriftian Purpofes of Tyrants and Ufurpers :
Recollect, pray, what I have faid concerning
Sermons and Prayers, and what is done by fome
Clergymen under Pretence of Preaching the
Gofpel.

Hor. I do, and can eafily fee, how Preachers, by a fmall Deviation from the Doctrine of
Peace, may infenfibly feduce their Hearers,
and, perverting the End of their Function, fet
them on to Enmity, Hatred, and all Manner of
Mifchief : But I can't underftand how Fafting
and Humiliation fhould further, or be made
any ways inftrumental to that Defign.

Cleo.

Cleo. You have allow'd, that the Grand Point in Armies, and what has been ever moſt labour'd among military Men, was to make them believe, that Heaven, that is, the Deity they adore, was of their Side; and it is certain, (as I have hinted before) that how widely ſoever Men have differ'd in their Sentiments concerning the inviſible Cauſe, or the Worſhip it requires, they have all agreed in this; and the Uſe that has been made of Religion in War has ever had a palpable Tendency this Way. The Word Faſting, indefinitely ſpoken, ſounds very harſhly to a Man of a good Stomach; but, as practiſ'd religiouſly among *Proteſtants,* it is hardly an Emblem of the Thing it ſelf, and rather a Joke than any grievous Penance: At leaſt in *England,* by keeping a Faſt-Day, Men mean no more, than Eating their Dinners three or four Hours later than they uſed to do, and perhaps no Supper that Night: Which is a Piece of Abſtinence, that is ſo far from being likely to have an ill Effect upon the Strength or Spirits of Men in Health and Vigour, that there is not One in Fifty, whom it will not render more briſk and lively the next Day. I ſpeak of People that are not in Want, and who, of dainty or courſer Fare, eat as much

much every Day as their Appetite requires.
As for Humiliation, it is a Word of Courſe.
Faſt-Days, bar the Abſtinence already mention'd, are kept no otherwiſe, than the *Sunday*
is. In the Army of the Rebels, the Chaplains
perhaps preach'd and pray'd ſomewhat longer
on thoſe Days, and read a few Chapters more
in the Bible, than was uſual for them to do
on a Sabbath-Day. But that was all.

Hor. But you have allow'd, that many of
the *Roundheads* were ſincere in their Religion,
and that moſt of the Soldiers, tho' they were
bad Chriſtians, were ſtill Believers. It is unreaſonable to think, that the Solemnity of
thoſe Days, and the continual Shew of Devotion they were ſpent in, ſhould have made no
Impreſſion upon a conſiderable Part of ſuch a
Multitude, as you your ſelf ſuppoſe their
Army to have been. Where a great Number
of the Vulgar, who believe Hell-Torments and
Fire Everlaſting, are forced to hear, firſt
their Lives laid open, and their Iniquities diſplay'd, and, after that, all the terrible Things,
that the Parſon can ſay of Eternal Miſery, it
is impoſſible, that many of them ſhould not
be affected with Fear and Sorrow, at leaſt for
that Time : However, this is beyond all Diſ-
pute

pute, that the mildeſt Remonſtrances that can be made on that Head, will ſooner diſpoſe Men to Melancholy, than they will to Chearfulneſs.

Cleo. All this while you take that for granted, which I told you long ago was notoriouſly falſe; *viz.* That in Camps and Armies, the plain Doctrine of *Chriſt* is delivered without Diſguiſe or Diſſimulation: Nay, I hinted to you juſt now, that if Repentance was preach'd among Military Men, as might be expected from Chriſtian Divines, Soldiers would be in Danger of being ſpoil'd by it, and render'd unfit for their Buſineſs. All knowing Clergymen, at firſt Setting out, ſuit themſelves and their Doctrine to the Occupations, as well as Capacities of their Hearers: And as Court Preachers ſpeak in Praiſe of the Government, and applaud the Meaſures of it, ſhade the Vices of Princes and their Favourites, and place their Merit in the handſomeſt Light it can be ſeen in; ſo Divines in Armies ſpeak up for the Juſtice of the Cauſe they are engaged in, and extol the Generals to the Skies; cajole and curry Favour with the Troops, and flatter more particularly the reſpective Regiments they belong to. There is not a Chaplain in an Army, who is not perfectly

fectly well acquainted with the Duty of a Soldier, and what is required of him. Therefore they preach Christianity to them, as far as it is consistent with that Duty, and no farther. Where they interfere, and are clashing with one another, the Gospel is set aside. The Politician must have his Business done: Necessity is pleaded, and Religion ever made to give Way to the Urgency of Affairs. There is a vast Latitude in Preaching; and Clergymen often take great Liberties: Being as much subject to Errour and Passion as other People, they can give bad Counsel as well as good. Those, who are pleas'd with a Government, we see, preach one way; and those who are not, another. Above Half the Time of the last Reign, a considerable Part of the *English* Clergy exhorted their Hearers to Sedition, and a Contempt for the Royal Family, either openly or by sly Inuendo's, in every Sermon they preach'd: And every Thirtieth of *January* the same Church furnishes us with two contrary Doctrines: For whilst the more prudent and moderate of the Clergy are shifting and trimming between two Parties, the hot ones of one side assert with Vehemence, that it is meritorious as well as lawful for the People, to put

their

their King to Death whenever he deferves it ; and that of this Demerit, the Majority of the fame People are the only Judges. The Zealots on the other, are as pofitive, that Kings are not accountable for their Actions, but to God only; and that, whatever Enormities they may commit, it is a damnable Sin for Subjects to refift them. And if an impartial Man, tho' he was the wifeft in the World, was to judge of the Monarch, whofe unfortunate End is the common Topick of the Difcourfes held on that Day, and he had no other Light to guide him, but the Sermons of both Parties, it would be impoffible for him to decide, whether the Prince in Queftion had been a fpotlefs Saint, or the greateft Tyrant. I name thefe obvious Facts, becaufe they are familiar Inftances of our own Time, to convince us, that the Gofpel is no Clog which Divines think themfelves ftrictly tied to. A fkilful Preacher, whether it be a Faft, or a Day of Rejoycing, always finds Ways to purfue his End, inftills into his Hearers whatever he pleafes, and never difmiffes an Audience, before he has acquainted them with what he would have them know ; let the Subject, or the Occafion he preaches upon, be what they will.

will. Befides, an artful Orator may mention frightful Things without giving Uneafinefs to his Hearers. He may fet forth the Enormity of any great Sin, and the Certainty of the Punifhment, that is to follow it. He may difplay and dwell upon the Terrors of the Divine Vengeance for a confiderable Time, and turn at laft all the Weight of it upon their Adverfaries; and having demonftrated to his Audience, that thofe whom they are to fight againft, or elfe the great Grandfathers of them, have been notorioufly guilty of that Wickednefs, which is fo heinous in the Sight of Heaven, he may eafily convince Believers, that their Enemies muft of Neceffity be likewife the Enemies of God. If any Difgrace has happen'd to an Army, or fome of the Men have misbehaved, a wary Preacher, inftead of calling them Cowards, will lay all the Fault on their little Faith, their trufting too much to the Arm of Flefh, and affure them, that they would have conquer'd, if they had put greater Confidence in God; and more entirely rely'd on his Affiftance.

Hor. And fo not have fought at all.

Cleo. The Coherence of thefe Things is never examin'd into. It is poffible likewife for

a

a crafty Divine, in order to rouse a liftlefs
and dejected Audience, firft to awaken them
with lively Images of the Torments of Hell
and the State of Damnation, and afterwads feem
happily to light on an Expedient, that fhall
create new Hopes, and revive the drooping Spirits of a Multitude ; and by this Means
the Courage of Soldiers may often be wrought
up to a higher Pitch than it could have been
rais'd, if they had not been terrify'd at all. I
have heard of an Inftance, where this was perform'd with great Succefs. Provifions had
been fcarce for fome Time; the Enemy was juft
at Hand ; and Abundance of the Men feem'd
to have little Mind to fight ; when a Preacher,
much efteem'd among the Soldiers, took the
following Method: Firft, he fet faithfully
before them their Sins and Wickednefs, the many Warnings they had received to repent, and
God's long Forbearance, as well as great Mercy,
in not having totally deftroy'd them long ago.
He reprefented their Wants, and Scarcity of
Provifion, as a certain Token of the Divine
Wrath, and fhew'd them plainly, that labouring already under the Weight of his Difplea-
fure, they had no Reafon to think, that **God**
would connive longer at their manifold Neg-
lects

lects and Tranfgreffions. Having convinced
them, that Heaven was angry with them, he
enumerated many Calamities, which, he faid,
would befal them ; and feveral of them being
fuch, as they had actually to fear, he was
hearken'd to as a Prophet. He then told
them, that what they could fuffer in this
World, was of no great Moment, if they could
but efcape Eternal Punifhment; but that of
this (as they had lived) he faw not the leaft
Probability, they fhould. Having fhewn an
extraordinary Concern for their deplorable
Condition, and feeing many of them touch'd
with Remorfe, and overwhelm'd with Sorrow,
he chang'd his Note on a Sudden, and with an
Air of Certainty told them, that there was ftill
one Way left, and but that one, to retrieve all,
and avert the Miferies they were threaten'd
with; which, in fhort, was to Fight well, and
beat their Enemies; and that they had Nothing
elfe for it. Having thus difclofed his Mind to
them, with all the Appearances of Sincerity,
he affumed a chearful Countenance, fhew'd
them the many Advantages, that would attend
the Victory; affured them of it, if they would
but exert themfelves ; named the Times and
Places in which they had behaved well, not
                                        without

without Exaggeration, and work'd upon their Pride fo powerfully, that they took Courage, fought like Lions, and got the Day.

Hor A very good Story ; and whether this was preaching the Gofpel or not, it was of great Ufe to that Army.

Cleo. It was fo, politically fpeaking. But to act fuch a Part well, requires great Skill, and ought not to be attempted by an ordinary Orator ; nor is it to be tried but in defperate Cafes.

Hor. You have fufficiently fhewn, and I am fatisfied, that as Fafting is practifed, and Preaching and Praying may be managed by wary Divines, Care may be taken, that neither the Strictnefs of Behaviour obferved, nor the Religious Exercifes perform'd on thofe Days, fhall be the leaft Hindrance to military Affairs, or any ways mortify or difpirit the Soldiers ; but I cannot fee, what Good they can do where Religion is out of the Queftion. What Service could an *Atheift*, who knew himfelf to be an Arch-Hypocrite and a Rebel (for fuch you allow *Cromwell* to have been) expect from them for his Purpofe ?

Cleo. I thought, that we had agreed, that to pleafe the Party he was engaged in, it was

his

his Intereft to make a great Shew of Piety a-
mong his Troops, and feem to be religious
himfelf.

Hor. I grant it ; as I do likewife, that he
throve by Hypocrify, raifed Enthufiafm in o-
thers by Counterfeiting it himfelf, and that
the Craft of his Clergy was many ways inftrumental to his Succeffes : But a fkilful Hypocrite, and able Politician, would have made no
more Rout about Religion, than there was Occafion for. They had Praying and Singing of
Pfalms every Day ; and the Sabbath was kept
with great Striƈtnefs. The Clergy of that Army
had Opportunities enough to talk their Fill to
the Soldiers, and harangue them on what
Subjeƈt they pleafed. They had fuch a Plenty
of Religious Exercifes, that it is highly probable, the greateft Part of the Soldiers were
glutted with them: And if they were tired
with what they had in Ordinary, what good
Effeƈt could be expeƈted from ftill more Devotion Extraordinary ?

Cleo. What you named laft is a great Matter. What is done every Day is foon turn'd
into a Habit ; and the more Men are accuf-
tomed to Things, the lefs they mind them ;
but any Thing extraordinary roufes their Spirits
and

and raifes their Attention. But to form a clear
Idea of the Ufe and Advantage, a mere Politician, tho' he is an Unbeliever, may reafonably expect from Faft-Days, let us take into
Confideration thefe two Things: Firft, the
Grand *Defideratum* in Armies, that is aim'd
at by Religion, and which all Generals labour
to obtain by Means of their Clergy : Secondly,
the common Notions among Chriftians, both
of Religion and of War. The Firft is to perfuade the Soldiers, and make them firmly believe, that their Caufe is Juft, and that Heaven
will certainly be on their Side; unlefs by
their Offences they themfelves fhould provoke it to be againft them. All Prayers for Succefs, Thankfgivings for Victories obtain'd, and
Humiliations after Loffes received, are fo many
different Means to ftrengthen the Truth of
that Perfuafion, and confirm Men in the Belief of it. As to the Second, Chriftians believe,
that all Men are Sinners; that God is Juft,
and will punifh, here or hereafter, all Trefpaffes
committed againft him, unlefs they are atton'd
for before we die ; but that he is likewife very
merciful, and ever willing to forgive thofe, who
fincerely repent.   And as to War, that it is,
as all human Affairs are, entirely under his Direction,

rection, and that the Side whom he is pleased to favour, beats the other. This is the general Opinion, as well of those who hold a Free-agency, as of those who are for Predestination. A cursory View of these two Things, the Notions Men have of Providence and the Grand Point to be obtain'd in Armies, will give us a clear Idea of a Clergyman's Task among Military Men, and shew us both the Design of Fast-Days, and the Effect they are like to produce.

Hor. The Design of them is to gain the Divine Favour and Assistance ; that's plain enough; but how you are sure, they will have that Effect, I can't see.

Cleo. You mistake the Thing. The Politician may have no Thoughts of Heaven : The Effect I speak of relates to the Soldiers ; and is the Influence, which, in all Probability, Fast-Days will have upon Believers, that assist in the keeping of them.

Hor. What Influence is that, pray, if it be not Religious ?

Cleo. That they will inspire, and fill the Men with fresh Hopes, that God will favour them and be of their Side. The Reputation of those Days, that they avert the Divine

vine Wrath, and are acceptable to Heaven, is, in a great Meafure, the Caufe, that they have this Influence upon the Men. The Heathens harbour'd the fame Sentiments of their Publick Supplications; and it has been the Opinion of all Ages, that the more Solemn and Refpectful the Addreffes are, which Men put up to the Deity, and the greater the Numbers are that join in them, the more probable it is, that their Petitions fhall be granted. It is poffible therefore, that a Politician may appoint Extraordinary Days of Devotion, with no other View than to chear up the Soldier, revive his Hopes, and make him confident of Succefs. Men are ready enough to flatter themfelves, and willing to believe, that Heaven is on their Side, whenever it is told them, tho' they have little Reafon to think fo. But then they are unfteady, and naturally prone to Superftition, which often raifes new Doubts and Fears in them. Therefore Common Soldiers are continually to be buoy'd up in the good Opinion they have of themfelves; and the Hopes they were made to conceive, ought often to be ftirr'd up in them afrefh. The Benefit that accrues from thofe Extraordinary Days of Devotion, and the Advantages expected

pected from them, are of longer Duration, than juft the Time they are kept in. With a little Help of the Clergy, they are made to do Good when they are over ; and two or three Days or a Week after, the Ufefulnefs of them is more confpicuous than it was before. It is in the Power of the General, or any Government whatever, to have thofe Days as ftrictly kept, to outward Appearance, as they pleafe. All Shops may be order'd to be fhut, and Exercifes of Devotion to be continued from Morning till Night ; nothing fuffer'd to be bought, or fold during the Time of Divine Service ; and all Labour as well as Diverfion be ftrictly prohibited. This having been well executed makes an admirable Topick for a Preacher, when the Day is over, efpecially among Military Men ; and Nothing can furnifh a Divine with a finer Opportunity of commending, and highly praifing his Audience, without Sufpicion of Flattery, than the Solemnity of fuch a Day. He may fet forth the outward Face of it in a lively Manner, expatiate on the various Decorums, and Religious Beauties of it ; and by faithfully reprefenting what Every body remembers of it, gain Credit to every Thing he fays befides. He may magnify and

fafely

fafely enlarge on the Self-denial, that was
practifed on that Day ; and, afcribing to the
Goodnefs and Piety of the Soldiers, what in
his Heart he knows to have been altogether
owing to Difcipline, and the ftrict Commands
of the General, he may eafily make them believe, that greater Godlinefs and a more general
Humiliation never had been feen in an Army.
If he has Wit, and is a Man of Parts, he'll find
out Quaint *Similes.* Happy Turns, and Plaufible Arguments, to illuftrate his Affertions,
and give an Air of Truth to every Thing he
advances. If it fuits with the Times, he'll
work himfelf up into Rapture and Enthufiafm, congratulate his Regiment, if not the
whole Army, on the undeniable Proofs they
have given of being good Chriftians, and with
Tears in his Eyes wifh them Joy of their
Converfion, and the infallible Tokens they
have received of the Divine Mercy. If a
grave Divine, of good Repute, acts this, as he
fhould do, with an artful Innocence and
Chearfulnefs in his Countenance, it is incredible what an Effect it may have upon the
greateft part of a Multitude, amongft whom
Chriftianity is not fcoff'd at, and Pretences to
Purity are in Fafhion. Thofe who were any
ways

ways devout on that Day, which he points
at, or can but remember that they wiſh'd to
be Godly, will ſwallow with Greedineſs whatever ſuch a Preacher delivers to them; and
applauding every Sentence before it is quite
finiſh'd, imagine, that in their Hearts they
feel the Truth of every Word he utters. We
are naturally ſo prone to think well of our
Selves, that an artful Man, who is thought to
be ſerious, and harangues a vulgar Audience,
can hardly ſay any Thing in their Behalf,
which they will not believe. One would
imagine, that Men, who gave but little Heed
to the Religious Exerciſes they aſſiſted at,
could receive no great Comfort from their
Reflection on that Day, ſuch, I mean, as were
tired to Death with the Length of the Prayers, and almoſt ſlept as they ſtood the greateſt
Part of the Sermon; yet many of theſe, hear-
ing the Behaviour of the Army in General
well ſpoken of, would be ſtupid enough to
take Share in the Praiſe; and remembring the
Uneaſineſs they felt, make a Merit of the very
Fatigue they then bore with Impatience.
Moſt of the Vulgar, that are not averſe to Religion, have a wild Notion of Debtor and Cre-
ditor betwen themſelves and Heaven. Natural

ral Gratitude teaches them, that some Returns must be due for the good Things they receive; and they look upon Divine Service as the only Payment they are able to make. Thousands have made this Acknowledgment in their Hearts, that never after cared to think on the vast Debt they owed. But how careless and neglectful soever most of them may be in the Discharge of their Duty, yet they never forget to place to their Accounts, and magnify in their Minds, what little Time they spend, and the least Trouble they are at in performing what can but seem to have any Relation to Religious Worship; and, what is astonishing, draw a Comfort from them by barely shutting their Eyes against the frightful Balance. Many of these are very well pleased with themselves after a sound Nap at Church, whose Consciences would be less easy, if they had stay'd from it. Nay, so extensive is the Usefulness of those Extraordinary Devotions, appointed by Authority, in Politicks only, that the most inattentive Wretch, and the greatest Reprobate, that can be in such an Army, may receive Benefit from them; and the Reflection on a Fast-Day, may be an Advantage to him as a Soldier. For tho' he cursed the Chaplain in his Heart, for

preach-

preaching such a tedious while as he did, and wish'd the General damn'd, by whose Order he was kept from Strong Liquor such an unreasonable Time ; yet he recollects, that Nothing went forward but Acts of Devotion all the Day long; that every Sutler's Tent was shut; and that it was Six a Clock before he could get a Drop of Drink. Whilst these Things are fresh in his Memory, it is hardly possible, that he should ever think of the Enemy, of Battles, or of Sieges, without receiving real Comfort from what he remembers of that Day. It is incredible what a strong Impression the Face, the outward Appearance only of such a Day, may make upon a loose wicked Fellow, who hardly ever had a Religious Thought in his Life ; and how powerfully the Remembrance of it may inspire him with Courage and Confidence of Triumph, if he is not an Unbeliever.

Hor. I have not forgot what you said Yesterday of the obdurate Soldier ; and I believe heartily, that the greatest Rogue may build Hopes of Success on the Devotion of others, whom he thinks to be Sincere.

Cleo. And if the bare outward Shew of such a Day, can any ways affect the worst of an Army,

there

there is no Doubt, but the better Sort of them may get infinitely more Benefit by keeping it, and giving Attention to the greateſt Part of the Preaching and Praying that are perform'd upon it. And tho' in Camps, there are not many Men of real Probity, any more than in Courts ; and Soldiers, who are ſincere in their Religion, and only miſled in the Duties of it, are very ſcarce; yet in moſt Multitudes, eſpecially of the ſober Party, there are ignorant Well-wiſhers to Religion, that, by proper Means, may be raiſed to Devotion for a Time, and of whom I have ſaid, that tho' they were bad Livers, they often deſired to repent ; and would ſometimes actually ſet about it, if their Paſſions would let them. All theſe an artful Preacher may perſuade to any Thing, and do with them almoſt what he pleaſes. A bold Aſſurance of Victory, emphatically pronounc'd by a popular Preacher, has often been as little doubted of among ſuch, as if it had been a Voice from Heaven.

Hor. I now plainly ſee the vaſt Uſe that may be made of Faſt-Days, as well afterwards when they are over, as during the Time they are kept.

Cleo.

Cleo. The Days of Supplication among the Heathens, as I hinted before, were celebrated for the same Purpose ; but their Arts to make People believe, that the Deity was on their Side, and Heaven espoused their Cause, were very trifling in Comparison to those of Christian Divines. When the *Pagan* Priests had told the People, that the Chickens had eat their Meat very well, and the Entrails of the Victim were found, and that the Rest of the Omens were lucky, they had done, and were forced to leave the Belief of those Things to the Soldiers. But ——

Hor. You need not to say any more, for I am convinced, and have now so clear an Idea of the Usefulness of Extraordinary Devotions, and a great Shew of Piety, among military Men; I mean the Political Usefulness of them, abstract from all Thoughts of Religion; that I begin to think them necessary, and wonder, how great and wise Generals ever would or could do without them. For it is evident, that since the Prince of *Conde*'s and *Cromwel*'s Armies, such a Shew of Godliness has not been seen among any regular Troops, in any considerable Body of Men. Why did not *Luxemburg*, King *William*, Prince

Prince *Eugene,* and the Duke of *Marlborough* follow thofe great Examples, in modelling their Armies after a Manner that had bred fuch good Soldiers?

Cleo. We are to confider, that fuch a Shew of Piety and outward Devotion, as we have been fpeaking of, is not to be created and ftarted up at once, nor indeed to be made practicable but among fuch Troops as the *Huguenots* in *France,* and the *Roundheads* in *England* were. Their Quarrels with their Adverfaries were chiefly Religious; and the greateft Complaints of the Malecontents in both Nations were made againft the Eftablifh'd Church. They exclaim'd againft the Ceremonies and Superftition of it; the Lives of the Clergy, the Haughtinefs of the Prelates, and the little Care that was taken of Chriftianity it felf and good Morals. People, who advance thefe Things, muft be thought very inconfiftent with themfelves, unlefs they are more upon their Guard, and lead ftricter Lives than thofe, whom they find Fault with. All Minifters likewife, who pretend to diffent from a Communion, muft make a fad Figure, unlefs they will reform, or at leaft feem to reform every Thing they blame in their Adverfaries.

If

If you'll duely weigh what I have faid, you will find it impoffible to have an Army, in which outward Godlinefs fhall be fo confpicuous, as it was in the Prince of *Conde*'s or *Oliver Cromwel*'s, unlefs that Godlinefs fuited with the Times.

Hor. What peculiar Conjuncture, pray, does that require.

Cleo. When a confiderable Part of a Nation, for fome End or other, feem to mend, and fet up for Reformation; when Virtue and Sobriety are countenanced by many of the better Sort; and to appear Religious is made Fafhionable. Such was the Time in which *Cromwell* enter'd himfelf into the Parliament's Service. What he aim'd at firft was Applaufe; and fkilfully fuiting himfelf in every Refpect to the Spirit of his Party, he ftudied Day and Night to gain the good Opinion of the Army. He would have done the fame, if he had been on the other Side. The Chief Motive of all his Actions was Ambition, and what he wanted was immortal Fame. This End he fteadily purfued: All his Faculties were made fubfervient to it; and no Genius was ever more fupple to his Intereft. He could take Delight in being Juft, Humane and Munificent, and with equal Pleafure he could

oppref

opprefs, perfecute and plunder, if it ferved
his Purpofe. In the moft Treacherous Contrivance, to haften the Execution of his black-
eft Defign, he could counterfeit Enthufiafm,
and feem to be a Saint. But the moft enormous of his Crimes proceeded from no worfe
Principle,than thebeft of his Atchievements. In
the Midft of his Villanies he was a Slave to
Bufinefs ; and the moft difinterefted Patriot
never watch'd over the Publick Welfare, both
at Home and Abroad, with greater Care and
Affiduity,or retriev'd the fallen Credit of a Nation in lefs Time than this Ufurper : But all
was for himfelf ; and he never had a Thought
on the Glory of *England*, before he had
made it infeparable from his own.

Hor. I don't wonder you dwell fo long upon *Cromwell*, for Nothing can be more ferviceable to your Syftem, than his Life and
Actions.

Cleo. You will pardon the Excurfion, when
I own, that you have hit upon the Reafon
What I intended to fhew,when I ran away from
my Subject, was, that able Politicians confulr
the Humour of the Age, and the Conjuncture
they live in, and that *Cromwell* made the
moft of his. I don't queftion, but he would
have

have done the fame, if he had been born three or four fcore Years later. And if he had been to command an *Englifh* Army abroad, when the Duke of *Marlborough* did, I am perfuaded, that he would fooner have endeavoured to make all his Soldiers dancing Mafters, than he would have attempted to make them Bigots. There are more ways than one, to make People brave and obftinate in Fighting. What in *Oliver's* Days was intended by a Mafk of Religion and a Shew of Sanctity, is now aim'd at by the Height of Politenefs, and a perpetual Attachment to the Principle of mo-- dern Honour. There is a Spirit of Gentility introduced among military Men, both Officers and Soldiers, of which there was yet little to be feen in the laft Century, in any Part of *Europe*, and which now fhines through all their Vices and Debaucheries.

Hor. This is a new Difcovery; pray, what does it confift in?

Cleo. Officers are lefs rough and boifterous in their Manners, and not only more careful of themfelves, and their own Behaviour, but they likewife oblige and force their Men under fevere Penalties to be Neat, and keep them- felves Clean: And a much greater Strefs is laid

upon

upon this, than was Forty or Fifty Years
ago.

Hor. I believe there is, and approve of it
very much ; white Garters are a vaſt Addition to a clever Fellow in Regimental Cloaths ;
but what mighty Matters can you expect
from a Soldier's being obliged to be clean.

Cleo. I look upon it as a great Improvement
in the Art of Flattery, and a finer Stratagem to
raiſe the Paſſion of Self-liking in Men, than
had been invented yet ; for by this Means the
Gratification of their Vanity is made Part of
the Diſcipline ; and their Pride muſt encreaſe
in Proportion to the Strictneſs, with which
they obſerve this Duty.

Hor. It may be of greater Weight than I
can ſee at Preſent. But I have another Queſtion to aſk. The main Things, that in raiſing Troops, and making War, Politicians are
ſolicitous about, and which they ſeem altogether to rely upon, are Money, great Numbers,
Art and Diſcipline. I want to know, why
Generals, who can have no Hopes, from the
Age they live in, of thriving by Bigotry, ſhould
yet put themſelves to ſuch an Expence, on
Account of Religion in their Armies, as they
all do. Why ſhould they pay for Preaching
or

or Praying at all, if they laid no Strefs upon them ?

Cleo. I never faid, that the great Generals, you nam'd, laid no Strefs on Preaching or Praying.

Hor. But Yefterday, fpeaking of the Gallantry of our Men in *Spain* and *Flanders,* you faid, that you *would as foon believe, that it was Witchcraft that made them Brave, as that it was their Religion.* You could mean Nothing elfe by this, than that, whatever it was, you was very fure, it was not their Religion that made them Brave. How come you to be fo very fure of that ?

Cleo. I judge from undeniable Facts, the loofe and wicked Lives, the Generality of them led, and the Courage and Intrepidity they fhew'd on many Occafions. For of Thoufands of them it was as evident as the Sun, that they were very Vicious, at the fame Time that they were very Brave.

Hor. But they had Divine Service among them ; every Regiment had a Chaplain ; and Religion was certainly taken care of.

Cleo. It was, I know it; but not more than was abfolutely neceffary to hinder the Vulgar from fufpecting, that Religion was neglected

by

by their Superiours; which would be of dangerous Confequence to all Governments There are no great Numbers of Men without Superftition; and if it was to be tried, and the moft skilful Unbelievers were to labour at it, with all imaginable Cunning and Induftry, it would be altogether as impoffible to get an Army of all *Atheifts*, as it would be to have an Army of good Chriftians. Therefore no Multitudes can be fo univerfally wicked, that there fhould not be fome among them, upon whom the Sufpicion, I hinted at, would have a bad Effect. It is inconceiveable, how Wickednefs, Ignorance, and Folly are often blended together. There are, among all Mobs, vicious Fellows, that boggle at no Sin; and whilft they know Nothing to the Contrary, but that Divine Service is taken care of as it ufed to be, tho' they never come near it, are perfectly eafy in their Evil Courfes, who yet would be extremely fhock'd, fhould Any body tell them ferioufly, that there was no Devil.

Hor. I have known fuch my felf; and I fee plainly, that the Ufe, which Politicians may make of Chriftianity in Armies, is the fame as ever was made of all other Religions on the fame Occafion, *viz.* That the Preifts, who

pre-

preside over them, should humour and make the most of the Natural Superstition of all Multitudes, and take great Care, that on all Emergencies, the Fear of an invisible Cause, which Every body is born with, should never be turn'd against the Interest of those, who employ them.

Cleo. It is certain, that Christianity being once stript of the Severity of its Discipline, and its most essential Precepts, the Design of it may be so skilfully perverted from its real and original Scope, as to be made subservient to any worldly End or Purpose, a Politician can have Occasion for.

Hor. I love to hear you ; and to shew you, that I have not been altogether inattentive, I believe I can repeat to you most of the Heads of your Discourse, since you finish'd what you had to say concerning the Origin of Honour. You have proved to my Satisfaction, that no Preaching of the Gospel, or strict Adherence to the Precepts of it, will make Men good Soldiers, any more than they will make them good Painters, or any thing else the most remote from the Design of it. That good Christians, strictly speaking, can never presume or submit to be Soldiers. That Clergymen
under

under Pretence of Preaching the Gospel, by a small Deviation from it, may easily misguide their Hearers, and not only make them fight in a just Cause, and against the Enemies of their Country, but likewise incite them to civil Discord and all Manner of Mischief. That by the Artifices of such Divines, even honest and well-meaning Men have often been seduced from their Duty, and, tho' they were sincere in their Religion, been made to act quite contrary to the Precepts of it. You have given me a full View of the Latitude, that may be taken in Preaching, by putting me in Mind of an undeniable Truth; *viz.* That in all the Quarrels among Christians, there never yet was a Cause so bad, but, if it could find an Army to back it, there were always Clergymen ready to justify and maintain it. You have made it plain to me, that Divine Service and Religious Exercises may be ordered and strictly enjoin'd with no other than Political Views; that by Preaching and Praying, bad Christians may be inspired with Hatred to their Enemies, and Confidence in the Divine Favour; that in order to obtain the Victory, Godliness and an outward Shew of Piety among Soldiers may be made serviceable to the greatest Profligates,

who

who never join in Prayer, have no Thoughts
of Religion, or ever affift at any Publick
Worfhip, but by Compulfion and with Reluctancy; and that they may have this Effect
in an Army, of which the General is an *A-
theift*, moft of the Clergy are Hypocrites, and
the Generality of the Soldiers wicked Men.
You have made it evident, that neither the
Huguenots in *France*, nor the *Roundheads* in
England could have been animated by the
Spirit of Chriftianity; and fhewn me the true
Reafon, why Acts of Devotion were more
frequent, and Religion feemingly more taken
care of in both thofe Armies, than otherwife
is ufual among military Men.

Cleo. You have a good Memory.

Hor. I muft have a very bad one, if I could
not remember thus much. In all the Things I
nam'd, I am very clear. The Solution likewife, which you have given of the Difficulty I propofed this Afternoon, I have Nothing to object to; and I believe, that skilful Preachers confult the Occupations as well
as the Capacities of their Hearers; that therefore in Armies they always encourage and
chear up their Audiences; and that whatever
the Day or the Occafion may be, upon which
they

they harangue them, they feldom touch upon mortifying Truths, and take great Care never to leave them in a Melancholy Humour, or fuch an Opinion of themfelves or their Affairs, as might lower their Spirits, or deprefs their Minds. I am likewife of your Opinion, as to artful Politicians; that they fall in with the Humour of their Party, and make the moft of the Conjuncture they live in; and I believe, that, if *Cromwell* had been to Command the Duke of *Marlborough's* Army, he would have taken quite other Meafures, than he did in his own Time. Upon the whole, you have given me a clear Idea, and laid open to me the real Principle of that great wicked Man. I can now reconcile the Braveft and moft Gallant of his Atchievements, with his vileft and the moft treacherous of his Actions; and tracing every Thing, he did, from one and the fame Motive, I can folve feveral Difficulties concerning his Character, that would be inexplicable, if that vaft Genius had been govern'd by any Thing but his Ambition; and, if following the common Opinion, we fuppofe him to have been a Compound of a daring Villain and an Enthufiaftical Bigot.

Cleo.

Cleo. I am not a little proud of your Concurrence with me.

Hor. You have made out, with Peripicuity, every Thing you have advanced both Yeſterday and to Day, concerning the Political Uſe, that may be made of Clergymen in War; but, after all, I can't ſee what Honour you have done to the Chriſtian Religion, which yet you ever ſeem ſtrenuouſly to contend for, whilſt you are treating every Thing elſe with the utmoſt Freedom. I am not prepared to reply to ſeveral Things, which, I know, you might anſwer: Therefore I deſire, that we may break off our Diſcourſe here. I will think on it, and wait on you in a few Days; for I ſhall long to be ſet to Rights in this Point.

Cleo. Whenever you pleaſe; and I will ſhew you, that no Diſcovery of the Craft, or Inſincerity of Men can ever bring any Diſhonour upon the Chriſtian Religion it ſelf, I mean the Doctrine of *Chriſt*, which can only be learn'd from the New Teſtament, where it will ever remain in its Purity and Luſtre.

F I N I S.